A Boy I Once Knew

A Boy
I Once Knew

What a

Teacher Learned from

Her Student

by Elizabeth Stone

Algonquin Books of Chapel Hill

2002

Published by
Algonquin Books of Chapel Hill
Post Office Box 2225
Chapel Hill, North Carolina 27515-2225

a division of
Workman Publishing
708 Broadway
New York, New York 10003

Published simultaneously in Canada
   by Thomas Allen & Son Limited.
Design by Anne Winslow.

Library of Congress Cataloging-in-Publication Data
Stone, Elizabeth, 1946–
      A boy I once knew : what a teacher learned from her student /
by Elizabeth Stone.
         p. cm.
      ISBN 1-56512-315-8
      1. Vincent, d. 1995.   2. Gay men—United States—Biography.
3. AIDS (Disease)—Patients—United States—Biography.
4. Teacher-student relationships—United States.   I. Title.
      HQ75.8.V53 S76 2002
      305.38'9664'092—dc21   2001056529

10 9 8 7 6 5 4 3 2 1
First Edition

In some instances, to preserve the privacy of people in Vincent's life, names and other identifying details have been changed.

For my family

A Boy I Once Knew

The dead are flat. They stand
Impassively in rows like dominoes
Until they lean and one by one they fall.

RACHEL HADAS
"In the Grove"

THE BELL RANG THE first thing in the morning, even before the coffee was on. At my front door was the mailman, who handed me a large carton, its return address in blue block letters telling me it was from Vincent in San Francisco. This was odd. In the twenty-five years since I had been Vincent's ninth-grade English teacher at New Utrecht High School, he had never sent me anything but a Christmas card, though he had rarely missed a year. The last card—"Van Eyck's *Gabriel*," it said on the back—was still propped up on a bookshelf in my living room. As usual, it didn't say much, just "Dear Elizabeth" above the printed message and "Love, Vincent" below, but on the back, he'd drawn a circle around "Gabriel," the name of my younger son, so I knew he'd chosen the card for me.

When you're a teacher, some students burst out at you immediately, most emerge gradually, and a few don't want you to see them at all. By December, Vincent had never raised his hand, and although his serious brown eyes met mine from time to time, when I called on him, he merely shrugged.

It was a gray day in Brooklyn, and I'd assigned my English class O. Henry's "The Gift of the Magi," set on a long-ago Christmas Eve in Manhattan. It was about Jim and Della, young newlyweds who wanted to give each other the perfect Christmas present. They had very little money, and those who read all the way through knew that they did find the right gifts for each other, but only after Jim pawned his heirloom gold watch to buy Della the jewel-rimmed tortoiseshell combs she'd so admired, and Della cut and sold her long hair so she could buy Jim a platinum watch fob.

It was a touching story, and as the kids thudded their textbooks onto their desktops and shuffled around for the right page, I waited, curious as to what it had meant to them. At twenty-two, I was still a very new teacher, nervous and chronically overprepared, so the night before, I had written up a long list of questions to get the discussion going. But before I could ask even one of my questions, Vincent shot his hand up into the air. Then without waiting for me to call on him, he announced that he hated the ending, just *hated* it.

"How could anyone write something so stupid?" he said, his eyes flashing indignantly. "They spent all that money on presents that turned out to be useless, and they probably can't even exchange them."

Vincent glared at me as if their predicament might be my fault. At fourteen, he was slight and dark, with bony arms, pointy features, and a lock of hair that wouldn't stay out of his eyes. Now he flung his head in a way that was part hair management and part annoyance.

I was startled by his passion. "Do you think Jim and Della felt the way you do?"

Before Vincent could answer, Freddy Murphy, who had been waving his arm like a windshield wiper in a storm, spoke up. "I think they felt bad, but maybe Della can wear the combs even with short hair." He was a small boy with glasses who sat right in front of Vincent.

Vincent scowled at the back of Freddy's head, while Freddy, oblivious to this show of disapproval, happily continued. "Or maybe Jim can return the combs and get his watch back."

At this, Vincent rolled his eyes. "That's dumb," he muttered.

Freddy was a small round cheerful sort, whose two

small round cheerful parents had shown up to meet me a few weeks earlier at New Utrecht High School's Open School Night as had most of the parents, or at least mothers, of the kids in the class. Vincent was one of the few whose parents had not shown up. No note from them, no explanation from him.

Despite their different styles, Freddy was the only person I had ever seen Vincent talk to. They didn't seem to be friends, but with each lacking the rambunctious ease of the other boys, they appeared to be less uncomfortable with each other than with anyone else.

The class was now silent. "Any other thoughts?" I asked.

Another student raised her hand. "Well, maybe what really matters to them isn't the present but that they showed how much they loved each other."

That was the point of the story for most readers. Not for Vincent, though. Now he raised his hand so vigorously that I thought it would yank the rest of his body up with it. "That's ridiculous!" he said, pronouncing it *ree-diculous*. "If you love someone, you want to get them something they really want." He stopped for a second. "And you want them to get you something you really like, too." Clearly, giving and receiving carried a charge for him. He flung his head back again.

Vincent's intensity brought the class to life that day and made me look closely at him for the first time. When the bell rang, he came up to my desk to rail about the

ending of this "stupid story" at greater length. He stayed
so long that he had to rush to his next class.

That was how my relationship with Vincent had begun, and now, twenty-five years later, here I stood in my
living room, holding this carton from him.

"Don't you want to know what's in it?" said my husband, Reamy, prodding me.

I did, and so with me in robe and bare feet and with
Reamy and our son Gabe flanking me, I slit the box's
tape and lifted off the cover.

Inside were two or three stacks of red volumes, gold
lettering on their spines.

I think I instantly knew what those volumes were and
what their arrival meant, but I held the knowledge at
bay, like someone blocking off a smell by breathing
through her mouth. Before I was willing to know anything, I wanted Vincent to explain himself.

Slipped between the books, near the bottom of the carton was an envelope with "Elizabeth" written on it. Inside, on Vincent's letterhead, was a typed letter dated
February 10, six weeks earlier. It read:

Dear Elizabeth,

You must be wondering why I left you my diaries in my will. After all, we have not seen each
other in over twenty years. Our only contact is

our traditional Christmas cards, and yet I still feel connected to you.

Please be warned that some of the details can be raunchy and shocking. I probably should just destroy them, but they contain my thoughts, feelings, and desires of my life for the last ten years.

I was hoping that a book could be made into them and my only requirement is that my family's identity is never revealed. Also any profits should be given to my family, otherwise I leave all the details up to you.

I will understand if you decide not to accept this project. All I want is that they do not fall into the wrong hands.

One thing I will always regret is not seeing you one last time. Thank you.

Love

Vincent

Where Vincent should have signed his name—the part of him I knew best—there was only vast empty space. And that's when I understood: Vincent was dead. But how could he be? How could a living man tell me he was dead? And how could a dead man tell me he would "always" feel regret. It was impossible, and it made me dizzy. I set the box on the floor and sat down on the couch.

At the bottom of Vincent's letter were a few sentences in a neat, tight, and unfamiliar script, which I read aloud. "Vincent passed away the day I was to bring this typed letter for him to sign at the hospital. No one but you has the privilege of reading these diaries. Good luck, and please pray for Vincent that he rest in peace." It was signed "Carol."

"How did he die?" said Gabe.

"I don't know," I said. "Vincent's friend doesn't say." But AIDS crossed my mind right away. I'd long assumed that Vincent was gay, although he'd never said so. In all the time we'd exchanged cards, he'd never mentioned a wife or children or anyone else. During these years, Vincent had lived at only two different addresses on Clay. What I surmised, or at least hoped, was that Vincent was living a contented and companionable life with a vague someone else, a man somewhat like himself. As for me, in those same years, I had moved from the Village and then to the Upper West Side of Manhattan. Ten years ago, we'd left the city altogether for a house with a big front porch set behind a dogwood tree in Montclair, New Jersey. All these years with scarcely a miss in the Christmas cards we tossed across the continent to one another.

But it occurred to me that maybe Vincent had not lived as I had hoped, and I wondered if Carol's request that I pray for Vincent to rest in peace went beyond convention. Had Vincent not lived in peace? I wondered as I returned the letter to its envelope. If there were any answers, they were in his box of diaries on my living room floor. But Vincent's death was new, my knowledge even newer, and the box suddenly felt to me like an open grave.

Still I had to know what happened. Scanning the spines, I found 1994 and 1995, took them out and skimmed the pages, feeling all the while like a grave robber. These were the last weeks of Vincent's life, and I squinted to keep out what I was trying to take in:

> If I can just make it to Christmas . . . it may be the last time I see my family. . . . Huffed and puffed my way up the hill . . . getting harder and harder. . . . so cold, so hungry, so angry . . . 112 pounds. . . . No Christmas cards. Bummer. . . . I get upset because the pretty people on TV are not in pain. I'm jealous of their happiness . . . so tired, so cold . . . cried myself to sleep . . .

can't speak. . . . hard to swallow. . . . can't use arm . . . Angela called . . . Sandra called . . . so concerned & mother and father ditto. 108 pounds . . . I wonder if they suspect their only son is a goner . . . now I know how Eddy felt . . . spoke with Adrienne. . . ."

And then the confirmation. "She knows I have AIDS."

———⊗———

NEW UTRECHT HIGH SCHOOL, where I first met Vincent, is in the Bensonhurst section of Brooklyn. It's a tidy neighborhood, now heavily Asian and Russian, but when Vincent was growing up, most of the students were Italian, as Vincent was, or Irish or Jewish. Some kids set out every morning from apartment houses, but most of the neighborhood was made up of small private homes set back from lawns each the size of a large beach blanket.

Even now, without a glance at the yearbook, I can remember at least half a dozen kids who were in Vincent's class and gave that class its character. There was Natalie, who insistently referred to the author of *A Doll's House* as "Isben." Then there was Charlie, short, blond, and handsome, who was going to be a TV cameraman like his father. Near him sat nervous Anthony, daily a one-man rhythm section with his finger-drumming, ballpoint-clicking, and heel-tapping. Off in a corner, when she wasn't cutting class, sat Jeannie, she of the Technicolor makeup, rolled-up skirts, gum wads, and fixed sullen scowl. And she surprised me on the very last day of class by dropping what turned out to be a very sweet card on my desk on the way out. "Don't read it till I'm out the door," she instructed me.

But after class on that chilly December day, it was Vincent I thought about as the subway clacked and grumbled its way back to Manhattan where I lived. The touching irony of the O. Henry story had been over his head, at least at the outset. Still, with Christmas only two weeks away, it was obvious that the story stirred up something personal for him. Was he was feeling the misery of a giver who desperately wants to please and fears he has failed? I didn't know.

"The Gift of the Magi" drew Vincent in, and the next day and the day after that, he sat straight up in his seat with that expression of his that was at once sweet, sour, and sorrowful. At the end of the class, the other kids filed out talking to each other with animation about the real concerns of their lives, while Vincent often stayed on to talk about the day's reading, even *Silas Marner*. ("It's not *Mariner*," I heard him tell Natalie irritably. "It's *Marner*! Silas *Marner*!") In all my five classes, he was the only person with any of the urgent but undefined hungers I remembered having when I was his age and starting at Madison High School a few neighborhoods away.

By the time spring came, Vincent and I had become pretty chatty. Sometimes he waited for me outside the building's main entrance at the end of eighth period so he could walk me to the subway, and I looked forward to seeing him there. I was lonesome at New Utrecht, maybe as much as he was. At twenty-two, I was closer in age to Vincent than to most of the teachers, and though I'd made two or three friends among the teachers, I didn't feel like I was part of the community.

Meanwhile, Vincent had become frankly curious about me. At what he thought were polite intervals, he pursued his suspicions, or possibly hopes, about my life beyond Bensonhurst, past and present.

"So you went to Berkeley right near San Francisco?"

"Yes," I said.

"And now you live in Greenwich Village?"

"Yes. First in the West Village and now in the South Village. You ever been there?"

"No."

Sullivan Street, where I lived in a newly renovated studio apartment, was in transition. The neighborhood was half SoHo already, filling up with newcomers like me, and half the frayed northernmost fringe of Little Italy, where the old women in black sat in front of their tenement buildings on the vinyl-covered chairs they dragged out of their kitchens, while down the street, in the park, the old men played the Italian bowling game bocce.

The faces of these old Italians were deeply familiar to me, even comforting. They reminded me of my mother's family, and especially my grandmother—all dark-eyed with the full rounded features common in Southern Italians. I had struck up acquaintanceships with a few. Millie made me "gravy"—tomato sauce—and Willie, the grocer next door, cashed checks up to twenty-five dollars for me. Louie with one was lung was a fixture at Willie's, passing his days on a chair in front of the soups, a perpetually doleful expression on his face. Whenever he saw me, he told me that I should quit smoking.

Those first two years after college were the worst years of my life. As a senior, I had expected to pour myself into an already arranged future—I was going to marry Mark and join him at Indiana University. He was already in graduate school there, as I would be in the fall. But for a whole host of horrible reasons, nothing had worked out the way I expected, and in the fall, I was the spilt milk I was crying over, a splash without shape or direction. I started graduate school at New York University, but it felt wrong, and after a few weeks of half-hearted attendance and lots of doodling in the margins of my notebook, I dropped out.

Over the course of the next year, looking for something to mop myself up with, I wandered through various jobs—welfare case worker, bookstore clerk, administrative assistant in a noble nonprofit organization. I didn't care about any of them, or at least not enough, and at 5:00 P.M. I went home to my apartment on Barrow Street, which I shared with a parade of roommates as lost as I was.

In the fall of the second year, a friend of mine called to tell me about an ad she'd seen in the *Times* that morning. A high school for Hasidic Jewish girls in the Borough Park section of Brooklyn was looking for an English teacher. I had nothing better to do, so I called right away, speaking with the principal, a rabbi, who asked me to come in for an interview as soon as possible. Two hours later, I found myself in a small shabby building on Fifteenth Avenue looking for the rabbi's office. It was a hot Indian Summer day, and there was no air conditioning inside, but the girls going to and fro in the hallway, who glanced at me curiously, wore long sleeves, opaque white stockings, and skirts that came down to their calves.

The rabbi waved me to a seat across from him in his stuffy cluttered office. Hot as I was, he had to be feeling it more, with his long bushy beard, *payos,* and yarmulke. He was dressed in layers of black, except for his white shirt closed at the collar without any tie.

"We need an English teacher right away," the rabbi

explained in heavily accented English. Then he squinted at me with an expression I took to be disapproving—I was dressed conservatively in a beige suit, but now that I was seated, my knees showed—and he asked me only two questions: Did I have more "modest" outfits, and did I have a college degree? In that order. When I said yes to both questions, he gave a nod of satisfaction, and then he offered me the job. The salary was abysmal, and there were no health care benefits (unless, as I would say later on, one counted prayer), but I accepted.

The next day I began my life as a teacher. If I was a character in search of my own story, these girls turned out to be my authors. Because the Hasidim relied so heavily on reading and analyzing the Torah, the word —almost any word, really—was sacred to them, and teachers—all teachers, even me—were held in reverential regard. So the girls responded rapturously and ravenously to Shakespeare, Keats, Salinger, Fitzgerald, and anyone else I offered them.

After a month or two, Malki, Rachelle, and Shulamith, three exceptionally bright girls, came up to my desk after class one day and asked if they could do a senior thesis on an individual author. That June, they turned in twenty-page research papers that were better than most of those I've since read by college students. In those heady early months as I helped the girls shape their projects, I took their passion and intelligence personally, as if it were purely and simply a response to me and my teaching. By late fall, I was beginning to feel good, almost like the person they seemed to think they were talking to anyhow.

But another experience a few months later tempered my self-importance. One day, glancing out my living room window, I was startled to see three other senior girls in their long winter coats standing in front of my building looking up, pointing and talking to each other, trying to figure out which window might be mine. Pilgrims at a shrine. Groupies at a rock concert. All three were intelligent girls, friendly and diligent, but not girls I knew well. There was no way I could make sense of this kind of attention. What were they *doing* there?

Eventually, after a few circumspect conversations with them, during which I kept my knowledge of their Manhattan travels to myself, I figured it out: these were girls who wanted to go to college but whose parents had instead decided it was time for them to be married and had set out to make suitable *shidduchs,* or matches. This single furtive and certainly forbidden journey of theirs to Greenwich Village was part pilgrimage, but also part a farewell to their girlhood school days and part a small act of rebellion against their parents. I happened to be their teacher, and they liked me, or liked me well enough, but, more than I had initially understood, much of their attraction to me was because I was a member of what they called "the outside world," a world that they regarded with a push-pull mixture of fascination and contempt. Being their teacher, I was spared the contempt ("It's true you'll be our servant in heaven," said one, "but we'll treat you very very nicely."), but I soon realized that just about everything I was teaching them seemed alluringly dangerous. (One day, all aflutter, the rabbi had summoned me to his office to tell me that *under no circumstances* could I finish teaching a poem by Keats about which he knew nothing except its title, "The Eve of St. Agnes.")

Putting it all together, I glimpsed, just barely, that the dance creates the dancer. I saw, as I never had when I was a student myself, the glow that the role of teacher bestows, or can, on someone who just goes home and feeds her cats at the end of the day. At the end of the year, the seniors put eighteen photographs of me in their yearbook, seventeen of which the rabbi made them take out. I was flattered and grateful, but it didn't make me forget how my cats regarded me.

In all ways, my year among the Hasidim had been a good year. I picked myself up, and that summer I began graduate school again at New York University. Meanwhile, a job at New Utrecht at double the salary fell into my lap, and I took it.

Bensonhurst was only one neighborhood away from Borough Park, but I realized almost immediately that it was actually a world away, and that I had left the warmth of my Hasidic nest too soon. New Utrecht was big. It felt chilly and unfriendly, and I grew nervous all over again. The school secretary's voice rasped, and she didn't like anyone she didn't already know, or at least she didn't seem to like me. Early in the year, there was a bitter city-wide teachers' strike with the entire faculty and the raspy secretary on one side while I was on another. My students were sweet, and I liked them, but nothing I had to offer was anything that they really wanted.

And that's the way it went until Vincent erupted in a Christmas passion over O. Henry. He was as unaware of his gift to me as my Hasidic girls had been, but in his curiosity about books and in his poignant need to know what lay beyond Bensonhurst, he, too, looked at me as if I were already who I hoped to become, and thereby nudged me closer.

"This exact train goes right to the Village, doesn't it?" he asked one day as he walked me to the station, gazing upward at the elevated line longingly. "And from there you could go anywhere, right?"

"Right, anywhere," I said. I glanced at him. Bensonhurst was jail for him. He wanted to go someplace else and be someone else, but he was fourteen and he couldn't think

of how he could ever get out. I could practically see the
bars in front of his eyes. I was his teacher. I could help,
right? That's what I read in his expression.

Or maybe I imagined it. I told him about the time I'd
told a teacher of mine how I wanted to go to Berkeley for
college. She nodded, and the day before I left, she handed
me a letter that would introduce me to a friend of hers at
the university. "She'll look out for you," she told me.
When I got there, her friend agreed to meet me. She was
civil and cool, and I never saw her again, but by then I
was there, in California, and it didn't really matter.

On the final day of school in June, with textbooks col-
lected, tests marked, and report cards handed out, Vincent and I walked together to the B train one last time. I
was not coming back to New Utrecht. My Hasidic girls
had made me consider that teaching might really be part
of what I wanted to do with my life, and now Vincent
had confirmed it for me. Who knows what I would have
decided if he had not been in my class, but he was, and
so, having now finished my master's degree in English, I
was going to begin my Ph.D. In the fall, I would be a
graduate assistant teaching composition to a class of
NYU freshmen.

"Stay in touch with me?" I asked Vincent. It was more
a request than a question.

By way of reply, he opened up his notebook and extended it solemnly to me, as if it were a tray. I wrote down my phone number and address on the blank page. "Come visit me sometime," I said.

"Sullivan Street?"

"Sullivan Street."

THAT COULD'VE BEEN that, except that one Saturday afternoon, a few months later, someone buzzed me on my intercom.

I was not in the mood for visitors that day, and not expecting any, so I considered not answering. I was sitting at my window at a café table I had gotten for a dollar from a Bleecker Street restaurant going out of business, and I was reading for one of my courses quite happily.

The intercom buzzed again.

"Who's there?" I asked.

"It's me, Vincent!" a voice called back, gleeful even through the static.

My pique vanished. I buzzed him in, and in moments heard stampeding feet on the stairs. And then there he was at the top of the landing, out of breath, a warm if slightly hesitant grin on his face. I stood back to look at him. Still skinny, but not quite as scrawny. Dressed impeccably, too, in bell-bottoms and a T-shirt, Vincent looked really good. In back of him stood a boy his age that I didn't recognize.

"Oh," he said. "This is my friend, Robby." Robby and I nodded at each other. "He goes to Catholic school," Vincent added. We nodded again. Robby was a solid quiet boy with large sad eyes, eyes so light a brown they appeared almost yellow. He was at once so mournful and distinctive looking that I never forgot his face.

Vincent headed immediately for my rocking chair in front of the fireplace, and proceeded to rock back and forth with considerable zeal. Robby slunk over to the couch and poised himself glumly at its edge.

For the next half hour, Vincent sat, rocking and gulping down Mallomars and can after can of Coke from Willie's grocery. Robby, meanwhile, stayed motionless at the edge of the couch, eating nothing, drinking nothing, and saying nothing. Vincent was full of news—Freddy Murphy was in his geometry class, he himself hated math, Mr. Greenfield was his art teacher, art was great, and in a little while he and Robby were going to the movies at the Waverly a few blocks away on Sixth Avenue. Movies were great.

Soon they left, and for a few years after that, I didn't hear from Vincent at all. Then in the early 1970s, his first Christmas card came—on the front, a fat snowman with a red, green, and white scarf and a coal smile. The envelope bore a Brooklyn postmark, but there was no return address, and nothing written inside except four words:

"Dear Elizabeth" above the printed "MERRY CHRIST-MAS!" and "Love, Vincent" below it. The next year, and the year after that, the same thing.

But even without commentary from Vincent, there were clues about who he was becoming. After a year or two, the snowman was replaced by a Madonna and child from the Metropolitan Museum collection. The *z* in my name acquired a stylish slash through its midsection, and his lowercase *a* now looked like the ones on this page. Was Vincent in college? Was he working? He didn't say.

ON ONE OF THESE December days, somewhere in the mid-1970s, a Christmas card came bearing a San Francisco postmark and a return address on Clay, although Vincent didn't comment on his move. "So," I thought, as I rode the elevator up to my apartment, "he's finally made his great escape." I had finished my Ph.D. by now and moved to a larger apartment on West Ninety-ninth Street. I had a full-time job at Lehman College in the Bronx, my own brand-new used car, and a life I was happy with. I was teaching an extraordinary mix of students. In one class was Danny, nineteen, a black Orthodox Jew from the Bronx whose yarmulke sat on top of his full Afro and who planned to join the Israeli army after college; Dolores, a mother of two who was probably fifteen years older than I was, and who was just itching to leave her husband ("My B.A. is going to be my ticket out," she confided); and Milagros, a sedate young Puerto Rican woman who invited me to her Pentecostal church on the Lower East Side, where, in their ecstasy of worship, the parishioners spoke in tongues.

That December evening, after I got Vincent's card for the year, I sat for a while on my new couch with the pale yellow nubby fabric and butcher-block arms in my new living room, looking out at a cityscape that let me see as far as the Cathedral of St. John ten blocks away. I was thinking about Vincent, trying to see him as he was now, trying to imagine him in his new life, hiking up hills to new vistas. I knew San Francisco fairly well from my own undergraduate days at Berkeley, so I could loosely imagine Vincent in his new world. But even though I dressed him up in a blue suit and stuck a good leather attaché case in his hand, the Vincent I imagined was still a skinny boy with hair in his eyes and a nasal voice that hadn't entirely changed. Later that night when I began to write out my Christmas cards, I added a note telling him about my life now. At the bottom, I added a PS. I didn't mean to pry, I wrote, but could he write back and tell me a little about who he was now?

He didn't answer my question then, but he didn't forget it either. The next year his card arrived with his business card clipped to the top and a PS on the scant space at the bottom. The business card showed that Vincent was an underwriter at a Market Street insurance company, and the handwritten note at the bottom said he hated it, but that he loved traveling, especially in Europe, and taking photographs of his travels. I tried to imagine him at Chartres but I couldn't.

Then it was back to our usual transcontinental card toss, except for one fall when he sent me a postcard from Frankfurt, saying that he would be in New York for the holidays and maybe we could get together. But he didn't call and neither did I, though I knew it wouldn't have been difficult to track him down.

I never saw him again. Now he was dead of AIDS, and ten years' worth of his diaries were sitting in a box on my living room floor.

———

THERE WERE PEOPLE I could have called to learn more details about Vincent without reading another sentence of his diaries—Carol, whoever she was, had included her phone number as well as the number of someone named Sharon also in San Francisco. She'd also written down a Brooklyn phone number for Angela, who Carol said was Vincent's sister.

I didn't want to call any of these numbers. I didn't

know who these people were, or what I would say to
them, or how to explain who I was to Vincent. Whoever
Vincent had become, I wanted to encounter him on my
own. Then I supposed I would try to figure out what to
do next. Even without knowing what sort of man Vincent had grown into, I could understand him, or anyone,
simultaneously wanting to destroy the diaries he also
wanted preserved. But it was quite a leap to go from deciding against destruction to asking someone you hadn't
seen in twenty-five years to read thousands of pages—
handwritten pages—and then write a book about you.
It was strange. But it was also interesting.

As a woman in my prime, I didn't live intimately with
a recognition of my own mortality, not really. I felt there
was something unnatural, and therefore terrible and
poignant, about the death of someone younger than me,
someone I remembered as a boy barely out of childhood.
Vincent was fourteen the last time I'd seen him, now the
age of my son Paul. I also felt a voyeuristic curiosity that
drew me closer, and a fear of new death that pushed me
away. Beyond that? All I felt was a familiar clumsy con-
fusion that overcame me at difficult times and blunted or
obscured whatever emotions lay underneath, a sudden
winter snow covering the landscape.

For me, as I suppose for everyone, encountering death
qualified as difficult. My relationships with the two most

significant dead people in my life—my grandmother, whom I loved unambivalently, and my father, whom I didn't—were not good. I had never put it into words before, but now I did: death deadened me. When they died, I not only lost them, but it seemed to me I lost most of my own feelings for them. I certainly didn't want to be haunted by either one of them, but I did envy those people who now and then viscerally felt the living presence of the dead just over their shoulder, and felt it so strongly they were consoled.

I even envied those who had such vivid dreams of the dead that on awaking they were grieved anew. When I dreamt of my dead, they were flat and vacant, a reflection of me, the dreamer. They walked or talked, sat or stood, but whatever had made them who they were to me was bleached out.

When I thought about it, and when I looked at the varieties of loss in the lives of those around me, I had so many questions. How do you forgive someone who leaves without any warning? Or get beyond the long slow death of someone you loved? How do you remain loyal to someone you loved passionately, yet let yourself love again? And how do you learn to get along with someone even if you didn't always when he or she was alive? How do people feel the dead as real once they're gone? How do they summon a recollection substantial enough to bring a genuine smile? I heard all these questions from people I knew, but the last three were the most pressing questions for me.

There was another problem, too: I didn't think my mother would live much longer, and if she did, she would not continue to be who she was. She was disappearing a little bit every day now. It wasn't her aging—she'd always been tiny and now she was just tinier. It was that her keen intellect and memory for recent events were being nibbled and gnawed from within. "My head feels filled with cotton balls," she told me one day. That was about a year before Vincent's diaries arrived. Now when I visited her in Brooklyn, in the house where I'd grown up, she gave me updates. "Trying to remember is like trying to hold water in my hands," she told me as we ate lunch in the kitchen. "My memories slip between my fingers."

Soon my mother as I'd known her would be gone altogether, her mind, her spunk and humor vanishing a few steps ahead of her body. If I didn't figure out a way to remember who she'd been all these years of my life, I'd lose her altogether and some of myself as well.

THE FIRST IMPORTANT DEATH to me was my grandmother's, my mother's mother. She died suddenly of a heart attack late one winter afternoon when I was seventeen, two hours after a visit to my house, which I had missed. It was dark when my Uncle Joe, her eldest son, came and sat on the piano bench in our living room telling my mother, my father, my sister, and me the details.

My sister, Ginny, was the first to understand, and she cried right away.

"Don't be silly!" said my mother turning to Ginny, anger and fear in her voice. "It's not true." But then she knew it was true, and she cried, too.

Then Uncle Joe dissolved in tears. My father tried to comfort all three, circling them as, uncharacteristically, he bestowed fluttery pats and hugs not at all up to the task.

I got up and walked into the kitchen on someone else's legs. The coffee cup my grandmother had drunk out of that afternoon was still upside down in the dish drain. I stuck my finger in the cup to see if it was still wet. I wanted it to be wet because it would connect me to her still in the act of living, but it wasn't. I tore a piece of paper from my mother's grocery list and started writing about my grandmother's coffee cup, an act I remember only because years later I found the scrap of paper at the bottom of a dresser drawer. I wanted the words to be a portal to her and they weren't.

This was the death of someone I loved. The first day of

my grandmother's wake, my first wake, was right before
Valentine's Day. Flowers seemed to be called for, and I
wanted to buy some for her myself.

On that late winter Wednesday afternoon, right before
taking the bus to the funeral home where my parents,
aunts, uncles, and cousins were all going to gather, I
went to a florist on Flatbush Avenue near my bus stop
and told him I wanted to buy some flowers.

"What kind of flowers?" he asked, his pale fingers
splayed flat on the glass counter.

I didn't know. "Maybe red roses? Maybe some white
ones?"

He showed me a whole glass case full of flowers.

"What kind of arrangement?"

I didn't know that either.

Suddenly he put together what he thought of as two
and two, and flashed a coyly knowing smile at me. "Oh,
I see," he said. "A bouquet for a special someone?"

I froze. I could see where his thoughts were going, but
I couldn't think of how to reroute them. Instead, with no
known feelings of my own to anchor me, a twisted reflection of his coy grin spread over my face as I nodded
yes, feeling horrified and lost. He made a bouquet of red
and white roses. Then I got on my bus and sat all the
way to Snyder Avenue, on my lap the smooth white box
with its ebulliently curlicued cascade of red and white

ribbons. From inside the box, a cold waxen odor seeped out and around me.

After my grandmother's funeral, I remained numbstruck, unable to conjure up any but the most faded of images—a waxen old woman I didn't know lying in a coffin, dressed in pale blue, unfamiliar in pink lipstick. The lipstick was wrong, and the blue was wrong, too. She never wore blue. It was an alien colorized vision. At night, I dreamt of her sitting on a bamboo chair, pale, expressionless, and unmoving, neither alive nor dead. Without the right vivid images I couldn't find the feelings that went with them.

It shouldn't have been this way, and I don't know why it was. One of my uncles was an amateur photographer and over the years, on Christmas or Thanksgiving or Easter, he had taken dozens of photographs of my grandmother, the best of which he printed himself and distributed. Ours were in the album my mother kept in her bottom dresser drawer—all of them showing my grandmother as the beloved and smiling family hub that in fact she was, surrounded by her four daughters and two sons or dozen grandchildren. Any of these should have ignited my own active remembrance, but they didn't. After my grandmother's death, my aunts and uncles did lots of recollecting. But the Mamma they remembered with love and mirth—a woman who sang arias while cleaning her

stairs on her hands and knees, a woman who once pro-
tected my mother's teenage virtue by dumping a bucket
of water out the window and onto the heads of the
teenage boys hanging around her on the street below—
this was not Nana, the grandmother I'd known.

The grandmother I'd known gave me the silk hand-
kerchief embroidered with delicate purple and pink flowers her mother had given her when, at fifteen, she left her
island home just north of Sicily to come here and marry
my grandfather. My grandmother never saw her mother
again. Later on she gave me her cameo ring, which she'd
worn for so long the features of the ivory-carved woman
in the setting were rubbed away.

Eventually, I got some of my grandmother back, but
never all of her. What I was struggling to be able to do I
recently heard effortlessly expressed on a TV documentary by an employee at the L.A. Coroner's office who'd
had plenty of time to think about death. "There's an old
saying," he said, squatting at the feet of a father who had
just learned of his son's death, "You never lose the one
you love, if you love the one you lose." The father nodded, a tear skidding down his flat cheek.

OF COURSE I'D FACED other deaths, too—
friends, relatives, neighbors, colleagues—but in the af-
termath, it was the living I had reached out to, not the

dead. Now here was Vincent, announcing his own death to me, and asking me to resurrect him out of that white box as vitally and with as much dimension as I could— exactly the kind of imagination and feeling I was so deficient in. More, he was asking me to take the raw footage of his life over ten years and make him a story to live in.

And yet, I didn't feel I could put aside what was truly Vincent's deathbed wish without trying to save him from disappearing into oblivion the way a shoe tossed overboard sinks into the sea. For that reason alone, I wanted to be able to give him what he wanted, although I didn't know if Vincent's life would be of interest to me, much less to anybody else. Nevertheless, I felt that before I could decide anything, I needed to understand how Vincent had died. At least that. I wasn't ready to read his diaries, but since I was too uncomfortable to call his sisters, the diaries were all I had to turn to. So a day after the mailman rang my bell, I did.

It was a good thing, too. My need for information started us off on the right foot, nudging me into an engagement that felt real, neither sentimental nor self-conscious. What I needed from Vincent only he could give to me.

The next morning, once the house was empty for the day, I went back to the diaries, taking a half dozen out of the box. The ones from the earlier '90s were so much thicker than those that came later. Vincent's diaries doubled as scrapbooks, and they bulged with the stuff of his life, the mementos of his pleasures. While he was healthy, his life was so full he had needed to girdle the volume with a rubberband. As his life drained, his diaries thinned.

I started with his last entry, on February 9, the day before he died, and leafed through the pages backward. Then I opened to the end of 1994 and continued backward. Somewhere in that year, I found a photograph of a slight trim man with a considerable nose and dark mustache standing in front of a massive sandstone cupola and a placid lake dotted with ducks. He seemed to be about 5' 8", weighing maybe 140 pounds. He was dressed casually but smartly in jeans, a blue oxford shirt, and a sky-blue windbreaker, and he seemed very much at ease. Could this be Vincent?

It had to be. His hair was still in his eyes, or would have been if his eyes hadn't been masked by sunglasses. But he spoke out in his diary, answering my question at greater length than he had the day before. Yes, AIDS had killed him. And long before that, the fear of the disease had permeated his life, and the lives of his friends, in San Francisco. Whatever else these diaries were, they were journals of the plague years.

Nevertheless, Vincent lived his life and wrote about it.
And then he lived his dying and wrote about that, too.
Even skimming high over the words below, I could see
that he'd inventoried each new lesion, described each
new medication's side effect, decried each pound he lost,
mourned the steady drop in his T-cell count. He railed at
medical bureaucracy when he failed to qualify for one
experimental drug study because he was too well and
later was rejected from another because he was too ill.
By the fall of 1994, he had a hacking cough, constant
pain, and a disastrous T-cell count. And he was always
cold. But his Christmas card had come before everyone
else's as usual. How little I knew of him or his life.

I put 1994 back in the box and opened 1995 again.
Until the day before his death on February 10, Vincent
wrote in his diaries, documenting as much about his last
days as he could.

By January 26, weak and in pain, Vincent was finding
it almost impossible to leave the house, though a few
times he forced himself. When his friend Carol called
that day, he accepted her help reluctantly. "She brought
me 2 bottles ginger ale, gatorade. Did my dishes." In
gratitude, Vincent gave her a pair of earrings he had
bought her two days earlier on what turned out to be his
final independent trip out of his house. "She loved the
earrings."

On January 30, Carol had another idea. "She wants me to move to a lower floor. No. I'm happy in my own house." The same day, Vincent's sister Angela called. "She wants me to move back to NYC. No way."

Two days later, on February 1, Carol stopped by. "My house a mess," he wrote fretfully, in anticipation. The mess told Carol more than Vincent intended. "Carol contacted Angela," he wrote. "She & Sandra arriving tomorrow. Staying one week. Well, may be last time I see them." Had they known earlier that their brother was sick? Vincent didn't say.

Vincent's sisters thought maybe they could nurse him back to health, and came laden with herbs, minerals, and more, but Vincent couldn't swallow them. They cooked him scrambled eggs because they were soft, they gave him a little bell so he could ring for what he wanted (though the zeal with which he took to bell ringing left them with second thoughts), they scrubbed the kitchen, they did seven loads of laundry. While Vincent watched videos of Gilda Radner and Barbra Streisand in concert, they watched Vincent. Sometimes Vincent watched them, too—Angela, then Sandra, then Angela again—often with a beatific lingering smile they first found unnerving, but later soothing. He was grateful for them and their efforts to be "cheery and . . . strong for me."

"It is so weird waiting to die," he wrote on that last

Monday, the sixth. Now he was in a hospital bed, and his handwriting was jagged and woozy, a maimed version of what it had been six weeks earlier on my Christmas card. "I can't speak, use my hands, barely walk, cannot eat, I'm wasting away, and here I am in a hospital with tubes coming out of my arms and nose." With a wryness I would discover was typical, he added, "I am not very happy."

He had brought his diary to the hospital with him? It was my first glimpse of how passionate and perhaps how desperate his connection to these books were. "God, how I hate hospitals," Vincent wrote. "Poked me w/needles, taking my blood, blood pressure, temperature every ten minutes. I wish I was dead." But on Tuesday, he was inexplicably discharged. Some insurance problem. "I'm expected to drag an oxygen tank up and down my stairs. I don't think so." He decided that when his sisters left, he would go into a hospice.

On Wednesday the eighth, two days before his death, Vincent was back in the hospital, and again his diary was with him. It—and the other volumes—were much on his mind, especially arranging for their safe passage from his life into mine. "Sharon will mail diaries to Elizabeth," he resolved.

By now, due to what his doctor characterized as nerve damage, Vincent had lost almost total use of his hands and arms, so his writing was almost indecipherable. Each time I lured a word out of hiding, I felt a sense of victory, but it was slow going.

He knew his handwriting was deteriorating because on February 1, for the first time and maybe the only time, he wrote with me in mind as a reader. That was the day he had dragged himself to the medical center to see his doctor. "Examined [unreadable] charts," he wrote. "Nothing they can do unless I develop pneumonia." As he had written it, I couldn't read the last two words. But over those words, in another color ink (from the pen he used the following day) he had written "develop" and "pneumonia" so they were legible. His do-over, I knew, was for me.

A few days later, Vincent composed his only letter to me—the one in the carton—to make sure I understood what he wanted. "He whispered to Angela to come closer," Sandra later told me. "We both did, and he told us to make sure you received his journals. We looked at each other as if to say, 'Who the hell is Elizabeth Stone?'" Then he dictated to Angela the letter Carol would type and I would find amidst his diaries. "Gave her letter to type to Elizabeth," wrote Vincent in his next-to-last entry. "Should [have] done it myself while I was still able."

On the eighth, he spoke by phone with his mother

in Brooklyn. "She knows." She made Vincent promise to come home for his birthday in May, and he said he would.

On Thursday the ninth, he made what would be his last entry, which, like the others, was almost indecipherable to me, though mysteriously clear when I came to it again in sequence. By then I guess I had earned the right to read it. That day, Vincent made a trip by van to a clinic to get a CAT scan. He could only (and barely) crawl on his hands and knees, and initially he refused to go. But his doctor had called, telling Vincent that what could be learned from his CAT scan might later help others, and so Vincent had gone.

"Van brought us to appt. Another scan. I am so weak that Sandra had to help [me] get dressed. Waiting for a prescription, a security guard tried to kick me out. Thought I was a vagrant. On way home had to pee. Opened up van door & took a leak. It is amazing what one will do when one does not care. Dr. wants me to enter UC Med. I'll never see my house again. I'm not taking any more medicines. I just want to get it over with."

Those were the last words he wrote. The next day, he was dead.

Now, it was six weeks after his death, and his letter and the carton of diaries had reached me.

Are you not . . . forever whispering into the cosmos
   what all those other diaries shall forever whisper
   from their cupboards?
I was, I was—I am.

THOMAS MALLON
A Book of One's Own

DO OTHER PEOPLE'S DIARIES sing a siren song to everyone? Even as a child, diaries offered me the thrill of trespass, the discovery of secrets, the hope of special access, an intimate glimpse of another life. Once, I found a yellowed Brooklyn telephone directory in the middle of a careless musty pile near the boiler in the basement of my childhood. Inside were typewritten sheets taped to the pages. It was a diary my mother had kept as a teenager. For the next few days, I stole down to the boiler room to spy on her past. When she caught me, she burnt the diary—or at least that's what she told me—keeping her past mysterious to me. I must have felt guilty. I remember nothing of what I read.

My mother's daughter, I kept diaries of my own on and off till I was in my early thirties. Camouflaging them was a major priority (what if someone was as nosy as I was?) so I avoided using anything that looked like a diary. I almost never reread them, but I still had them, all of them, lined up on an out-of-the-way shelf in my study.

At first, I wrote by hand in notebooks. Then I switched to a typewriter and taped in the pages. Later I stored my entries in a black binder. Even later, I wrote on the computer, but I didn't like that at all. My own words were on the other side of the glass, beyond my reach. It was like visiting them in jail.

Only my very first diary—which I started when I was fourteen—actually looked like a diary. I took it off the shelf and blew off the dust. It was pale blue vinyl with the words "DEAR DIARY" on the cover and below them a girl with a pony tail reading a diary (her own? someone else's?) that also said "DEAR DIARY" on its cover.

The diary came with a clasp and a key I had long ago lost, but the clasp had never been much of a deterrent anyhow, nothing that my younger sister couldn't have cut with a pair of blunt scissors. Every night, I took the diary out of my night table drawer, sprawled across my bed, and wrote almost always to the bottom of the page. Partly I used it to practice what I took to be stylistic sophistication, the way a child in her mother's heels might mince her wobbly way toward a full-length mirror. ("I hope this shall be my best year yet," I wrote on my first day as a diarist, New Year's Day. "I shall truly try to make it so.")

But I didn't have anything to be sophisticated about, really, so I generally fell back on confiding what I ate that day or writing in code, the key to which was cleverly concealed on the last page of the diary. By mid-summer, I had a serious crush on Richard, the cousin of the girl next door. He was dark and brooding with a full under-lip, and in my diary, my longing for Richard and my ac-counts of our every encounter eclipsed my interest in food.

That summer, Richard and I sometimes used to meet at dusk in my backyard or on top of my peaked garage roof, in the back, where neither his aunt nor my mother could see us out their kitchen windows. On one of those evenings, Richard and I kissed. Suddenly, a kiss seemed part of a language I knew how to speak. Fluently. More enraptured than ever, I confided as much to my diary. On another evening, when Richard and I were sitting on the steps of my back porch, he told me he didn't think I re-ally liked him. He was just fishing, but I believed him, and was so hotly eager to be revealed to him that I ran up to my night-table drawer for my diary. I handed it to him, unlocked and spread open, and sat and watched him as he fingered the pages. When he handed it back, he had a funny look on his face.

This morning, as I put the blue vinyl diary back on its shelf, I understood what Richard might have felt that night—revelation could be risky not only for the revealer but for the confidant. Had Vincent known how high the stakes were? Had he known that if I lost the boy I knew and didn't like the man I found, I'd leave him as trapped in his diaries as he'd once been in Bensonhurst, only this time with no chance of escape?

I didn't know why Vincent had picked me to read his diaries. But in the end, I decided I would read them all the way through from start to finish. I had to find out what had become of the skinny kid I had known. We were like some surreal O. Henry couple, I thought, as I went downstairs to bring Vincent's carton up to my study. Vincent could share his life only by losing it, and I could get to know the man, but it might cost me the boy.

FOR SEVERAL WEEKS, the carton of Vincent's literary remains stayed in the corner of my study with the top firmly on. I wasn't ready to read yet. Meanwhile, I altered my exercise routine. Usually, I do step aerobics in my bedroom while I watch mindless action movies like *The Falcon and the Snowman* or *The Rock*. But for a week or two, I worked out to a six-part documentary with lots of San Francisco footage on the early history of AIDS lent to me by my filmmaker friend, Deb Wasser, who had been involved in its making. I was in training, not only to get a better sense of AIDS, but to look at Vincent's world, as much as possible, through his eyes.

Only in late April when spring light had fully taken over the study did I approach the carton. I moved it into the middle of the room, sat down on the floor next to it, and took off the top. Then I took out Vincent's diaries, laid them all out on the floor in neat rows of three, and counted them. There were fifteen of them altogether.

I found a mostly empty green notebook of my own lying on a shelf. On the first blank page, I made an inventory of Vincent's diaries, listing them in order:

    1984—purple travel
    1985—blue regular
    1986—red small
    1987—black regular
    1988—red regular
    1989—red regular
    1990—red regular
    1991—red regular
    1992—red regular
    1992—blue travel [October–November]

    1993 — red regular
    1993 — paisley travel book [May–June] [Dec]
    1994 — red regular
    1994 — spiral tan travel [Sept–Oct]
    1995 — red regular

At first I read nothing, taking the rubberbands off his diaries and looking only at what Vincent had stashed between the pages—clues to the lost civilization of his life. Even from the most cursory glance, I could tell that he used the red diaries for his everyday life. The others were varied—notebooks or cloth-covered books with blank pages inside—and these he reserved for his travels. Most of his trips, I noticed, had taken place in the last three years of his life. This was someone determined to live as fully as he could for as long as he could.

Tucked in the diary, I found dried flower petals, mass cards for dead friends, and theater ticket stubs; I found stamps, Lotto cards, foreign currency, carbons of money orders and American Express receipts; I found names and phone numbers scrawled on a McDonald's napkin and torn bits of paper, a Eurail pass, two dried leaves (stuck in his diary the day he visited the Parisian cemetery Père-Lachaise), passes to museums in Germany, France, Spain, and Switzerland, and fortune cookie fortunes that must have struck him as apt. Proust and his madeleines.

I discovered something else, too. Some of the mementos had Vincent's name on them, but others belonged to someone named Jimmy. After a little more poking around, I figured out that Vincent was known by both names. An American Express receipt signed in Paris showed that his middle initial was J. For James.

For some people, souvenirs are the husk of experience, disposable and irrelevant. But Vincent saved even the flimsiest memento, as if the feathers, photos, and cookie fortunes in his diary were precious receptacles where he stowed his memories and their emotional power. In Vincent's earliest travel diary, though not later on, he taped every theater stub and bus ticket to the left page and wrote only on the right page. Did his own words evoke less for him than these tangible prompts?

Even that first day, going through Vincent's diaries, I found myself there, too. I was startled the way we often are when we unexpectedly see our own face uncomposed for the encounter in a mirror and thereby see it anew. I saw the Christmas card I'd sent Vincent so long ago—one with a navy blue background and white snowflake in which I asked him to tell me about himself. I'd repeated the request the following year, 1976, and I found that, too, in a letter Vincent had kept preserved in its envelope. I'd written it on the first letterhead I'd ever had designed, a pale tan bond with my name and address printed in a rich brown.

That was the year my father died of his third heart attack, and I gave that as the reason for a letter rather than a card. "It doesn't have anything at all to do with orthodox rules of mourning," I'd told Vincent, "but the year has felt different to me and I've just been doing (or not doing) what feels right to me."

I took my own diary for that period off the shelf and skimmed my entries. In truth nothing at all had felt right to me during that year. I had retreated to my apartment when I wasn't teaching and sat at the kitchen table, night after night, typing pages and sticking them in the black binder I was using. "I feel sad through the night when I sleep," I wrote three weeks after my father's death, "but I walk around all day with a blank feeling, even when I'm not deliberately thinking about Daddy, and about Daddy being dead. I don't think about him directly very often. It's just that I see hearses all the time."

I didn't tell anyone about my father because I didn't want to be washed out to sea in their expressions of feeling—sympathy, empathy, or anything. I didn't want to be offered stock phrases by anyone who hadn't known him. Except for anger, I was largely blank about my feelings, and I didn't want anyone filling in the blank for me. It was my blank.

Whatever tender feelings I might have had for my father disappeared into the fog as they had with my grandmother, but the anger remained. My father had been a difficult man. He was a rabbi's renegade son from the Lower East Side of Manhattan, who, to hear him tell it, turned his back on Judaism at fourteen because as he and his father walked to *shul* one Sabbath morning, his father told him no, Indians could not go to heaven.

Not long after that, he was expelled from Stuyvesant High School. He told me the principal made his mother cry and so he punched him in the nose and then ran away to Wyoming. There he learned how to mix paint, and then he came back. By day, he operated a small paint store in downtown Manhattan. Evenings he took acting classes and pursued a career in the theater. He and my mother had first met when he came to join (but refused to audition for) the small repertory company she belonged to. By the time I was born, my father had left acting and abandoned paint. I knew him as the owner of a few small job lot stores in downtown Manhattan about which he cared not at all.

At least, he didn't care about the business end. One of the stores had a small loft-style office in the back, complete with a microphone. As the lunch hour crowds milled about the bins of cutlery and shelves of dried spices, my father took to the mike and did his own in-house talk show.

His other passion was fishing. He patented a fresh-water fishing lure called the Phoebe, which I'm told is still sold, and a few years later, he developed an electric smokehouse (in which he hickory-smoked eels, and once, a Thanksgiving turkey, which nobody liked). He spent every free moment alone on his boat in Jamaica Bay fishing for bluefish or striped bass.

As a father he was perpetually disappointing, a whiskey drinker who began to marinate himself in alcohol in November, and kept at it with great dedication until the spring. By then he was so sodden he could no longer resist our efforts to hospitalize him so he could dry out. One of my most indelible childhood memories was watching Alec, the manager of one of his stores, standing in back of him on the stairway in our house, maneu-vering him up the stairs to a second-floor bedroom, atilt at a 45° angle, as if he were a large household appliance.

As long as he was alive, I had left off deciding—or knowing—what I really felt about him on the chance, on the hope, on the wish that he might redeem himself. His death from a heart attack did not come as a surprise to me. I had seen it coming six months earlier, the night my mother had driven him, at breakneck speed, to a hos-pital because his lungs were filling up with fluids and he couldn't breathe. The day he came home, I sat down in the living room with him and told him I loved him because at that very moment, on the verge of his departure, I found the exact vantage point from which, if I stood very still and didn't move my head, it was true. Or could be true.

When he died, I thought that the polls were closed and all I had to do was count up the vote, and that's what I'd written in my own diary soon after he died. I figured I'd learn how I felt once and for all. But someone had run off with the ballot box.

The anger that remained, though, was better than the complete blankness I had felt with the loss of my grandmother. Anger was a supple feeling, too, capable of both expansion and contraction, despite the obvious lack of new input from my father. It was the first time I understood that relationships with the dead are not entombed in amber, fixed forever as they were at the moment of another's death. The new input that changed my relation to my father came from me, especially after I had children of my own, both of whom I loved with an intensity I couldn't have predicted.

When I saw what parenthood actually entailed, I reevaluated both my parents. I saw that my mother really had done the best that she could, and I forgave her the rest. But I saw my father had not done much of anything.

My disappointment in him grew as I saw with so much pleasure Reamy's flexibility and grace with our sons over the years. He loved Paul and Gabriel, but he also saw them and recognized them. He made Paul the Minister of Silly Walks, bought them both chocolate-filled Advent calendars every year, and made them cinnamon toast, mixing together the spice and sugar just as his mother had, just the way they liked it. When either boy was sick, he was often the one who stayed home from work with them. Meanwhile, ten years after my father's death, my father and I were more estranged than ever.

I closed my own diary and put it back on the shelf and again picked up my long ago letter that Vincent had saved. I saw that I had also written:

> Someday, I might have to write a story about you. Every year, faithfully, for the last eight years you've sent me a Christmas card, and always it is enigmatically spare: "Dear Elizabeth (printed message) Love Vincent"—: "Isn't it strange," I always think, "this year the card is from California, and it's up to me to intuit the life that's going on from year to year for Vincent. But how does he remember to send a card—has he had one address book that long?

Or when he gets a new one and has to transcribe the old, does he enter my name reflexively, or does he think about it, pause for a moment, and then do it? I'm not altogether in the dark as to why eight years after the fact of New Utrecht Vincent is still sending me a card. He was bright, very bright, much more sensitive than most. I know in some ways there was a rapport between us that we both understood existed. . . . Someday I'm going to write a short story about him."

I remembered sitting at my kitchen table writing Vincent this letter, and I was struck that an event I so clearly remembered was one with resonance for Vincent as well. This fact, nearly twenty years old, was a brand-new piece of news to me, and I felt a sudden and surprising flash of connection with this man I didn't know.

Somehow, he had made sure my letter came back to me. Had that letter to him now become his letter to me? Was he now asking me to write a story about him? Telling me I would have to invent him in order to keep him alive in me? Hadn't that been what I had been suggesting, at least lightly, when I said in order to know him I might have to make up the details myself?

Aren't we always inventing people anyhow, even those

most fully revealed and standing right in front of us? We don't invent their ready laugh or their quick temper, their incisive intellect or their generosity with panhandlers, but our idea of a person is a gestalt, a psychic still life of selected qualities in arrangement. What qualities we place in the foreground or background, what we put in combination or take off the canvas isn't inevitable, and isn't what someone else would do. In that way, our idea of another person, or a character in a novel, or even of ourselves, is an act of imagination.

And although our sense of another is stable, it isn't necessarily permanent. Love turns frogs to princes, right in front of (or behind) our eyes. Some of us are better artists than others, more generous with our eye. Nevertheless, once created and installed, the person outside us seems indistinguishable from the one within.

And who can do otherwise? I thought again how, once upon a time, Vincent had helped me invent myself, even if he didn't know it. He had seen me generously, and I had become, at least in part, the person he had imagined.

So now, I sat on the floor of my study with that letter of his in my hand and thought about Vincent's own artistry. Out of a long-ago year in a classroom and a few letters, he had invented someone to whom he could entrust his most valued possessions and his most private thoughts. It was as much an act of trust as an act of desperation. I would never have handed my diaries over to anyone.

Vincent signed his will less than a year before he died, making only five specific bequests (the rest going to his parents). His books went to the San Francisco Public Library, and his CDs, record collection, and videos went to three different friends. But before them all came the disposition of his diaries. "I will understand if you decide not to accept this project," he had said in that letter in the white carton, as if we two were *Mission Impossible* characters. I got up from the floor of my study, and taped Vincent's letter to the window near my desk.

Then I turned to the pages in Vincent's diaries and began to read about his life, day by day by day, a journey that would take me a year.

As we discover, we remember; remembering,
we discover; and most intensely do we
experience this when our separate journeys
converge. . . . The memory is a living thing—
it too is in transit. But during its moment,
all that is remembered joins and lives.

EUDORA WELTY
One Writer's Beginnings

VINCENT'S FIRST DIARY WAS a small nondescript brown notebook, and he began it on a September morning in 1984, his first day in London. "Of course I did not sleep on the plane. Instead watched movie ('The Natural')," he wrote. "Slept all day. Up all night." When he woke up the next morning, his first trip was to the Tower of London ("very torrid past"), the blue ticket stub taped into his diary. His plans were open, and often he did not know where he'd be sleeping at the end of that day. By Christmas, he would make his way through England, France, Spain, Italy, and Greece.

Vincent had planned this adventure for months. When

he had saved up enough money, he quit his job (whatever it was, he never referred to it again) and took off.

Virtually everything that came his way was cause for celebration. "FINALLY DID MY LAUNDRY—YAAY!" he wrote one night that week. I had to laugh.

He had turned thirty that year ("Today I am 30½ yrs old," he wrote on November 10 from Calabria) and had been living in San Francisco ever since he'd gone there on vacation in September 1976 and loved it so much he wound up staying.

After that, he came back one or twice a year to visit his family in Brooklyn or to spend time on Fire Island with friends or to travel on the east coast—Washington D.C., Atlantic City, or Boston. Every September 25, he wished himself a happy anniversary.

He didn't write much about his daily life, but he seemed to have four or five friends at home whom he dreamt about or alluded to now and then.

One was an antiques dealer named Robert who loved anything Art Deco. He had once lived in San Francisco but now lived in Atlanta. Before Vincent left, Robert phoned him to tell him about a new boyfriend named Sam. Robert was smitten, but Vincent was dubious. Anyhow, despite occasional grumpiness about how high his phone bills were, Vincent liked talking to Robert because Robert always made him laugh.

Then there was Joey, a short, chunky, bubbly hospital administrator, and a steady friend in Vincent's life. Vincent had borrowed his suitcase for the trip but within days it had fallen apart. The two had met a few years earlier in an adult education photography class at City College. Joey asked Vincent for a date, but Vincent wasn't interested, and told Joey outright he was too fat. Anyway, he said, friends lasted longer than boyfriends did so why didn't they just become friends, and so they had.

Another was Eddy Cavello (Vincent often referred to him by both names) who did Vincent's hair, supplied him with marijuana, and appeared now and then in his dreams. He was gorgeous, with dark curly hair, and very quiet. Vincent never quite knew what Eddy was thinking because Eddy never said. He did know that Eddy had once been attracted to him, but Vincent was not attracted back. Somehow from there the friendship grew.

And finally there was Ronny, a long and lanky bartender originally from Honolulu, who sported shades and a goatee and whom Vincent first met at one of the gay bars where he hung out. Of the four friends, Ronny appeared the most often in Vincent's dreams, and he was the only friend Vincent bought a present for—a flamenco doll from Spain.

Vincent mentioned his sisters, Angela, Adrienne, and Sandra, more than any of his friends, both because of their frequent appearances in his dreams and because he was always buying them presents of one kind or another.

By Christmas, Vincent had been traveling for four months. During the day (generally after complaining how poorly he'd slept the night before) he was up and out early visiting every museum, cathedral, fountain, mountain, seashore, and garden he could find. Each evening back at his hotel, he'd tape the paper trail of the day's adventures on the left side of his notebook— including local bus tickets, hotel bills paid for with his American Express card, and ticket stubs from museums like the Louvre. The mementos looked exactly as they had the day Vincent placed them in the diary, but the tape was brown with age. By October, he was already on his second roll of tape. I could tell because it was narrower than the first.

His diary was as new to him as it was to me, and it showed in his entries—best pen, best handwriting, at least for a while, and much more circumspection in detailing his late night dalliances than he would have in the future. Sometimes when he wanted to go out and be "complete trash," he did, and sometimes he didn't. In Venice, "started following this cute boy around, but not sure of his intentions, so let him be." In Rome, he was up all night with Francesco. In Biarritz, it was Jean Louis. "Last day in Biarritz—last day in France," he wrote.

"Took last walk near plague." I did a doubletake. Was this grim prescience? No, Biarritz was on the coast. He had to mean *plage*—French for "beach."

For Christmas, Vincent was back in Brooklyn with his parents and sisters. On New Year's Eve, he watched *Gypsy* on TV in the house he'd grown up in. The next day, feeling restless, he took the B train to a bathhouse in the East Village. "Broke New Year's resolution #1 & played at St. Mark's," he confessed to his diary later that day. "Got a room. Felt weird & guilty since here it is the beginning of 1985 & already I am exposing myself. Better be careful, fool."

THAT CHRISTMAS, LIKE EVERY OTHER, Vincent and I had exchanged cards. As I read through his life in 1984 I was amazed at how little we had known about each other. By then, I was long finished with my Ph.D. I had specialized in the eighteenth-century British novel, but ultimately discovered I wanted to spend my time in this century. I continued teaching, but I had also become a journalist. I had a movie column in one of the women's magazines, but mostly I wrote profiles—of movie stars and madams, of Nobel Laureates and college presidents.

An article I wrote on growing up Italian American had made me curious about family stories, those little snips of fact and semifiction about family members, living and dead, that float in and out of familial conversations. I thought they were full of meanings and messages, and that year I was almost finished with a book about them.

By then, I had been teaching for fifteen years, the previous five as a journalism professor at Fordham University. As a beginner, I had run on passion, gratified by how much my students gave me. Now I was a more deliberate saleswoman, even performer. I was also teaching a wide range of students all in the same classroom— some were elderly ladies with buns and seamed stockings who treated me with the deference and formality of another age. Quite a few of my students were women my own age, and they were easy, conscientious, and determined to succeed. The eighteen year olds were still my regulars, recognizable always despite the changes in music, drugs, and politics. Somehow, I adapted and found my way, and every year or so, one or two students became friends.

My husband, Reamy, and I had met at a Christmas party in 1977. We stood at the dining room table sipping mulled wine and talking about *A Bintel Brief,* the stories of immigrant newcomers, which we had each just read. When we went out to dinner on a cold winter night a few weeks later, a young mother stopped us on Sixth Avenue right near the Waverly Theater and asked Reamy to keep an eye on her two-year-old son for a moment as she raced across the street to fetch a second child. As Reamy hunkered down and talked quietly to the cold worried little boy, I glimpsed what our lives together could be. A door opened, and we walked through it. By 1984, we had been married for six years and lived on the Upper West Side with our two-year-old son, Paul. Many of these broad strokes Vincent knew.

As I reeled backward in time, I saw that the week Vincent had been strolling through the Prado in Spain, Reamy and I had been sitting round the clock in a Manhattan hospital pediatric ICU hoping that Paul wouldn't die—from a bacterial infection, epiglottitis, for which, at the time, there was no preventive vaccine. At the hospital, his X ray had been misread and the three of us were sent home with reassurances, but Reamy and I knew so profoundly that something was wrong with our listless whispering child that we returned. My mother, who was especially close to Paul because she baby-sat for him while we were at work, drove from Brooklyn to the hospital as soon as we called her. She took one look at her first grandson, sedated into unconsciousness—a gnarl of tubes threading in and out of him, machines beeping and blinking around him—and she covered her face with her hands and sobbed. Children died from epiglottitis, but Paul was lucky. How do mothers and fathers go on after their child dies, even parents of a grown child like Vincent?

By spring 1985, I was pregnant with Gabe, a complicated pregnancy that kept me involved daily with doctors and hospitals. It was a difficult spring for Vincent, too. When he got back from Europe, it took him a month to find a new job. He hated working, but his money was running out. Plus he learned that his own doctor had AIDS. Meanwhile, swollen glands, real or imagined, kept him perpetually in front of his bathroom mirror poking, but now that he had no doctor, no money, and no medical insurance, he did nothing. Except worry.

By early July, I was in the hospital, depressed that my pregnancy was riskier and more uncertain than ever. Vincent was depressed, too, and not even marijuana helped him cope. By July 12, I was fine, but Vincent was feeling worse because of what was happening with Ronny, his bartender friend and recipient of the flamenco doll. "Bad news," he wrote, "spoke w/Ronny. He's got AIDS." When I read this, I was taken aback. I had begun reading Vincent's diaries knowing that I was going to have to face illness and death, but I was not prepared to face either one this soon. But here was Vincent already facing what I was so bad at facing.

Ronny had been undergoing tests for a month and Vincent had reported on all of them. "He showed me his predicted medical malfunctions. Very depressing," he wrote. Ronny was now too ill to tend bar, and he had no family in the area, only a mother in Hawaii who told him not to come home for Christmas when he told her he was ill. "He told me all the hassle of dealing with financial aid," probably Medicaid. "He's coping pretty well. Told me I'm his best friend."

In 1985, not much was known about AIDS, including how it was transmitted, and being friends with Ronny made Vincent nervous. "Invited him for dinner," he wrote a few days later. "It was OK though I felt uncomfortable about him eating over and sleeping in my bed. . . . I'll get over it."

By 1986, Ronny was sicker, and though Vincent thought of him often, he was also in flight from Ronny and frequently found excuses not to visit him. On May 5, after two weeks without any mention of Ronny in his diary, Vincent concluded the day's entry: "Attempted to go to gym. Changed mind. Oh, tried to reach Ronny. Shanti would not tell me where he is. They took my name & #. We'll see."

Shanti was one of the hospice programs offering not only medical care to men with AIDS but counseling to their friends. Through Shanti, Vincent was invited into one such group, and he joined, at least nominally. As Ronny grew worse, Vincent got more and more calls from Lee, one of the Shanti counselors. "Told him I did not want to see him," wrote Vincent after one such call. "We spoke a little on the phone."

Another two weeks went by with no mention of Ronny from Vincent.

By Sunday, May 18, Vincent was feeling guilty. "Got high. Determined to visit Ronny. Arrived about 1:00. Stayed until 2:30. Brought him plant & tape. He's the same. Wants me to be his executor. Home by 3:00. Tuna for lunch. Got a little drunk."

Two days later, on Tuesday the twentieth, Ronny was much worse. "Home, making dinner," Vincent wrote. "Phone rings. It's volunteer from Shanti. Ronny really sick. Should see him. Finish dinner. Call his home. He's doing better. See him tomorrow. Had dinner. Got call from Ronny's psychiatric nurse. Ronny's in hospital. Too weak. Gave me his room #. I'll visit him tomorrow," he wrote.

On Wednesday the twenty-first, Vincent fortified himself with a glass of wine and forced himself to visit. "I am greeted by a man who looks Hindu. He sits me down & explains that Ronny is resting and is having problems breathing. I should talk to him. His room is very dark. He makes funny noises with his throat. I call his name. No response. I stay for a few minutes. Then I leave quietly." Vincent often listed the events of his day, but he rarely described them at any length, especially the troubling ones, and he never reflected on them. I was surprised at his willingness to relive a moment I knew had terrified him.

On Thursday, the twenty-second, Vincent wrote in his diary late in the afternoon as soon as he came home from work. "Ronny died today at 2:10. I still haven't cried." For the first time, Vincent was trying to figure out how to mourn a dead friend, and how to remember him —and suddenly I was interested in a new way. Maybe I would learn something from him.

But no, Vincent was as inept at grieving as I was. The next day, sitting in his cubicle at his office, he was numb and jumbled, clumsy. Everything that could go wrong did go wrong, he thought, and he attributed it to how upset he was about Ronny. Before work, he had bought a blueberry muffin at a bakery near his office. When it came time to pay, he realized he had left the house with no money. By lunchtime, he wanted to go out and get drunk, but he stopped himself, staying in the office, planting himself in front of the office TV, and immersing himself in *All My Children*.

A few weeks later there was a memorial for Ronny: "I brought flowers," Vincent wrote flatly. "There were about 8 people. It was nice. We talked about Ronny."

But Vincent's grief stealthily wormed its way into his body, and soon hypochondria hit. One of his eyes was tearing and swollen, and after brooding about it, he found a doctor to consult. Nothing the doctor could find. Meanwhile, Vincent was always fatigued, and spent night after night at home, slumped down in the couch in front of the TV, too tired to make late-night sorties to Polkstrasse or any of the other neighborhood bars he liked.

When his favorite shows, like *Dallas,* weren't on, he watched videos from his ample collection. "I started watching 'Big Chill,'" he wrote one night of the film about friends who get together to mourn the death of a member of their group. "Got depressed." I thought he was not only depressed that evening but also depressed that whole spring and summer. I was hoping he'd call Lee, the hospice grief counselor, but he didn't.

The only way he regularly unburdened himself was through his diary. Although he rarely went into detail, Vincent was clearly attached to his diary. He wrote daily, never missing a day. Usually he wrote in his diary several times a day, sometimes completing after work a sentence he had left hanging in the morning—"I'm not happy about what I'll have to deal with when I get to work this morning, but actually the day went well"—or completing at bedtime a sentence begun after dinner. Even after reading through a few years, I wasn't sure what keeping a diary meant to him. He didn't seem to want it as an opportunity to tell a story or reflect on his life or analyze his experiences, and he didn't much think about his style. His writing was spare, even terse, a mnemonics of his experience.

Nevertheless, by now Vincent's pages were scrim to me. I could see right through them to him. The night of *The Big Chill*, I could see him clicking off the VCR with his remote and padding into his bedroom in the dark. When he crawled into bed wearing only his silk boxer shorts, the chill from his black satin sheets made him shiver for a minute, even in May.

In the mornings, if the garbage truck hadn't already awakened him before dawn, I could see him reaching to turn the alarm clock off at 7 A.M. His eyes were still closed to the day, but his arm was flung over the side of his bed, and his nervous thin fingers were feeling around on the floor for his diary and the pen he kept in it as if for part of his own body. Once he'd found the diary and opened his eyes, he'd sit up and write a few lines even before getting out of bed. He dressed fastidiously, sometimes changing his outfits a few times before leaving for work. By then, he was running late and he had to scramble—gulping down cold cereal or a yogurt before heading for the bus. And if the bus was crowded, he let it pass by. He had to have a seat.

However useless this knowledge was, it was intimate,

telling knowledge. The only people I knew this way and this well were members of my family.

And in fact I knew less about any of their dreams than I knew about Vincent's. From the first days of his diary, Vincent almost always began with what he'd dreamt the night before. Dreams, not words, were the realm in which he seemed to feel his emotions most vividly. Several times a week right now he was dreaming of Ronny. He rarely shared the details—"Had about a million dreams. Ronny was in one of them just watching in the background"—but at least I knew that at night, Ronny was with him.

After a few months, Vincent was ready to think about Ronny by light of day. His friend Sharon from work was good at sewing, and with her and a few other friends, Vincent made one of the very first panels for the AIDS quilt in memory of Ronny. I thought that he was lucky to have available a public and accessible way to commemorate Ronny. Even now, no other illness provides for its mourners this way.

Making the panel took Vincent weeks. First he had to choose the fabrics. I imagined him wandering the aisle of a dry goods store, picking up bolts of material, rubbing the fabric between his thumb and forefinger. I could see him standing before his own open closets looking at the patterns on shirts or old swimming trunks, wondering which one might be right for Ronny's panel. Did he ever run up against his own unwillingness to part with an item? Did he ever guiltily push his hesitation aside?

Finally the panel was done, and Vincent took a photo of it, slipping it into the diary for me to find it. "RON W. YEATES" it says in block letters stitched to a background of lush red and white tropical flowers. In the middle of the O in "RON" is a Coca-Cola emblem, which I figured was an allusion to Ronny's bartending work. The vertical bar of the first E in "YEATES" says "Hawaii," and the three horizontal bars have pictures of pandas. Did this point to his affection for bears? A photo Vincent took of Ronny during his illness shows him lying in bed, wan but turning his head, with an amused expression, toward a toy honey bear occupying the next pillow.

The finished panel was 6' by 3', and when Vincent next saw it, it was sewn to other panels of the same size, as part of the AIDS quilt. "Found Ron's panel," he wrote glumly, when he went to the first display of the AIDS quilt. "So unnoticeable."

I stopped here for the day. As I slipped the book back into its place on my bookshelf, I knew that he wanted me to do more for him than he had been able to do for Ronny.

⟨⟨⟨⟩⟩⟩

DURING THE FIRST TWO or three years of the diaries, my relationship with Vincent was new, and despite the blow of Ronny's death, Vincent was healthy and his life was pleasurable.

I also liked his sense of humor, a wry humor that he often turned on himself when yet another infatuation of his fizzled out. He told his diary over and over that he wanted true love, but actually love bewildered him. He was frightened of getting close to anyone, of being known, of accepting tenderness. He hated spending the night in an unfamiliar bed, but he didn't like an unfamiliar man spending the night in his, either. He was rarely interested in anyone he met, and when he was, he became obsessed, or opened himself far too wide, far too soon. He was lonely and starving for emotional contact though it was sex he endlessly dreamt about.

His experience with Rick was typical. The morning after Vincent and Rick went on their first date to the movies ("'Hair Spray.' Funny. Audience very gay"), Vincent woke up happy and excited. He and Rick had walked arm and arm, they laughed at the same jokes, and they sat in front of Rick's fireplace talking and kissing until way past midnight. Then Vincent went home. The next morning, back at his apartment, Vincent got up early and went to Tower Records because he wanted to buy Rick a present. There was a Gay Day parade later in the day and Rick had said he would call Vincent early in the afternoon so they could go together. After combing through show-tune CDs, Vincent settled on *Oklahoma*.

Back at his apartment, he spent the early afternoon circling a silent telephone. "Rick never called," he wrote later in the afternoon. "Oh, well."

In the early evening, though, Vincent was back at his diary to say that Rick had called after all. They got together, but by then Vincent had been left to stew in his own disappointment for five or six hours, and his feelings had gone tart on him. There was a third listless date, and then it was over. In general, malaise set in for Vincent by the end of the second date, anyhow. Whoever the new guy was, he was too dull, not good-looking enough, lived in a dump, wasn't rich enough.

Still, he had built himself a life, and he relished living in a world he felt he belonged in. He often took adult education courses, the best one a filmmaking course he took with Joey. He shot an eight-millimeter film that he wrote, directed, starred in, and edited, though what the story line was, he never said. Other semesters, he took night courses in gay literature and photography at San Francisco State University. Every year, he stuck into his diary ticket stubs from the annual gay film festival, and he dressed in his best tank top and shorts outfit for the Gay Day celebrations on the last Sunday in June. He participated in the Gay Games and was active in the endless fund-raisers for AIDS research.

HIS GREAT PASSION in life was getting on a plane and going somewhere—always with his diary—and he did so whenever he could find time and money. He loved Europe, especially Paris, where he had a friend he could stay with. Sometimes all he could manage was just a brief trip over a long weekend—to Yosemite or Lake Tahoe or Seattle, and he did that, too. Wherever he went, he went alone, and he preferred it that way. He said so.

As I got to know Vincent better, I realized how different our tastes were. His passions ran to *I Love Lucy* reruns, Philip Glass, and the *Smurfs,* and let's just say mine didn't. But in other important ways, I empathized with him. "I was attracted to a man," he wrote one day after he was back from the gym, "until I saw him reading a book by Nixon." Just what I might have said myself.

Vincent used lots of acronyms that I took pleasure in decoding. By their second or third appearance, I knew that KOW and AMC and GMAB stood for "knock on wood" and *All My Children* and "give me a break." BDD, which took me a little longer, turned out to be "big drug deal."

I also admired, and maybe even learned from, his ability to find pleasure in even the smallest experiences — lying on his roof on weekend afternoons with his eyes closed and letting the sun beat down on him, watching out his window as the fog rolled in from the bay, getting a good night's sleep. And as ever, he was a faithful and inspired gift giver. No milestone Vincent knew of — birthday, engagement, marriage, baby shower, or retirement — was ever allowed to pass uncelebrated. And he was honest with himself, which I admired. When he acted like a jerk, he knew it.

Then there was Vincent's Christmas passion. The young boy who had hated the ending to "The Gift of the Magi" fit as smoothly as the littlest Russian nesting doll into the man and made him recognizable to me. For Vincent, the holiday season began in October with the amassing of gifts for his sisters in Brooklyn. His packages to Brooklyn or to Robert in Atlanta were all mailed by early December and his Christmas cards went out no later than December 11. Of all the Christmas cards I received every year, Vincent's had always come first.

IT WAS DURING THIS getting-to-know-you period that I made my first appearance in Vincent's diary. I was startled at first — "Got Christmas card from Elizabeth Stone" — but finding myself there made me feel like less of an intruder. It also connected me to this man who was still in so many ways a stranger.

It was during this time, too, that I first began to have problems with Vincent, so much so that I sometimes had to stop reading.

It was all because of sex. It wasn't that I found his sex life "raunchy and shocking," as he had feared, or at least it wasn't only that. I found him carelessly self-destructive in ways I knew were going to kill him, and I couldn't stand it. I felt like a member of the chorus in a Greek tragedy, knowing the suffering and pain that lay ahead for him, unable to halt it. But whatever the chorus's foreknowledge did for them, mine left me infuriated. At Vincent. I hated watching a sexual Russian roulette I couldn't stop. Every time, I would wonder, "Was this the one?"

My worst experiences with Vincent came during the Christmas season of 1986, six months after Ronny's death. For reasons he didn't explain, Vincent was staying in San Francisco for the holidays instead of going back to Brooklyn.

Christmas was on a Thursday this year. Now it was the Saturday before, and to give the season its due, Vincent was having a dinner party for his friends that night, an act of expansive hosting that was unusual for him. In fact, this was the first time I'd known him to host anything. The night before, he was awake for hours, staring into the darkness, worrying, visions of alternate menus dancing in his head. When he drifted off, it was into strange dreams—in one, his sister Angela and her dog were on the high wire doing acrobatic tricks.

By 9 A.M., he was up and nervous about everything he had to do.

Before Vincent could begin, the phone rang. It was his best friend, Joey, the only person Vincent spoke to daily. Sometimes Joey's voluble cheer masked his serious social activism. Early on in the AIDS epidemic, he looked at what the San Francisco gay community needed, and decided they needed HIV-positive dating services as well as small informal neighborhood-based groups where men could gather and make sense of what was going on around them. So he rallied the right people and made it happen in his neighborhood. Joey didn't flinch from what was going on around him, but his zest never left him. He was a wild romantic, always madly in love. What he lacked in modulation he made up for in intensity. I tried to keep track of his boyfriends for a while, but there was such a steady parade that I quickly gave up.

When the phone rang, Vincent rarely answered it, lurking and circling instead, letting his answering machine screen calls that he then generally didn't intercept anyhow. In his diary, though, he made a daily list of who had called him, noting whether or not he'd picked up. When Joey called, Vincent always picked up, as he did now.

Joey was calling because he was all upset. He and his current boyfriend, Greg, had had a big fight. Yes, yes, Joey was still coming to Vincent's dinner party, but he was calling to say he didn't know if Greg would show up.

Then DDD called, and this time Vincent didn't pick up. He never picked up when DDD called, he never returned DDD's calls, and he hadn't invited him to his party either. DDD was the friend Vincent loved to hate —prosperous, a driver of flashy cars, a thrower of fancy parties, and, by Vincent's lights, a boaster of mammoth proportions. I never knew why DDD persisted, but he did.

By four o'clock, with all the frantic cleaning and furious shopping, Vincent hadn't started roasting his chicken yet. But in a sudden fit of anxiety, he decided he had to have flowers. Kahlúa and flowers. So he ran down four flights of stairs and down the two hills to the market on Polk. Then, bulky bags in hand, he ran up the hills and up the four flights again.

Joey was the first to arrive, knocking on the door at 8:30. No Greg. Too bad. But he handed Vincent a gift-wrapped box, his Christmas present. Inside was a beautiful blue bathrobe, Vincent's favorite color. Half an hour later, there was another knock at the door. It was Craig, a more casual friend of Vincent's who was trying to make a go of it as a model. He and Vincent sometimes had sex together when neither one of them had anything better to do, but basically they were just friends. Vincent was glad to see Craig tonight, and had a Christmas present for him, a Laura Nyro tape. Soon Eddy Cavello came, Vincent's friend and hairdresser and the only dinner guest about whom he hadn't complained to his diary at one time or another. In fact, Eddy was the only friend Vincent had who never seemed to irritate him. For Christmas, Eddy gave him a hit of speed.

Despite Vincent's early case of nerves, his dinner party went well. The only thing that bothered him was that he had cooked too much food. Eventually, Joey and Craig left, and Eddy stayed around to help Vincent wrap up food and wash the dishes. Vincent was personally fastidious, someone who set aside every Saturday morning to clean his kitchen and bathroom ("clean, clean, clean!" he'd write), not someone who could leave dirty dishes in the sink overnight.

Finally even Eddy was tired, so he left. It was well after midnight, but though Vincent had slept so badly the night before, he wasn't tired at all. It was the speed, he thought, jotting the perception in his diary as he sat in his very clean kitchen. It had left him wired and wide awake. To unwind, he went out to a few bars he liked on Polk, and had a couple of drinks. Vincent loved the Polk bars, he'd told Joey, because there he could be a "star." At the more upscale bars in the Castro District, Vincent felt less self-confident, maybe even a little out of his element.

After two drinks, Vincent went to "the peeps," a dirty bookstore where you could have quick and anonymous sex with strangers in adjoining booths. This night, he met a man named Al, and they "played," and then after that, he ran into Jack, whom he'd met once before. They also "played," and afterwards traded phone numbers, a bit of conventional politesse that rarely led to anything more.

But to Vincent's pleasure and surprise, a few days later Jack called, and they made plans to get together again. On Christmas Day, Vincent joined Joey and his boyfriend, Greg (by now they'd made up), at a Chinese restaurant for dinner and they all had a good time. Stuck in the diary for that day was a pale pink slip from a fortune cookie reading, "You are just beginning to live."

His date with Jack right after Christmas ended unusually for Vincent, with Jack spending the night. Jack used a condom, and the next morning they had sex again. "He fucked me without a rubber," Vincent wrote. I slammed the book shut, flung it into a desk drawer where I didn't have to see it, slammed the drawer shut, and left Vincent stranded in solitary.

If there was a time I was tempted to stop reading, this was it. Reading Vincent's diaries took time, real time. During these months, there were books I wasn't reading, articles I wasn't writing, and new courses I wasn't preparing. In diary time, I'd known Vincent for a few years now, and I didn't always like him. He could be a gold digger or worse. Once he'd met a guy at a bar who offered him $150 to come home with him. He hedged about saying whether he'd accepted, but in my less charitable moments, I thought that he probably had. Despite the fact that he'd told me his diaries were a record of all his "thoughts, feelings, and desires," frequently they were nothing of the sort. Often, his entries were opaque and unreflective, and more concerned than necessary with his bowels. All too often, he kept his diary—and hence me—at as much of a distance as he did all his friends (except for Joey, who had enough emotions for both of them).

I ventilated about this at night to Reamy as we cleaned up after dinner.

"So give it up," he said. "You don't have to read his diaries."

• • •

I CONFESS WITH SOME embarrassment that although months had now passed since Vincent's carton of diaries had arrived, I had made absolutely no attempt to get in touch with Vincent's sister Angela. How was I going to explain why her brother had left me his diaries when I really didn't know? And what in the world was I going to say to her about some of the discoveries I had been making about her brother and the way he lived his life? One day, though, a letter from Vincent's sister Adrienne arrived in the mail. "Hopefully you're still living at this residence," she began, "otherwise a complete stranger has gotten their hands on my brother's precious journals!" She and her sisters were troubled that they had never heard from me. Had I even received them? What was going on? What was I going to do with them?

I called Adrienne that day, omitting my current estrangement from her brother and the reason for it. She, like Angela, whom I soon spoke with, was a little wary, but ultimately they were willing to go through with whatever their brother would have wanted. They missed him terribly and all dreamt about him often, too. Adrienne told me Sandra would be calling soon, too, and she did. In the course of these conversations, I noticed all of them referred to him as Jimmy. They'd always called him

Jimmy, never called him anything else. It was his most intimate and tender name for himself. Once or twice Vincent had used "Jimmy" when he was consoling himself or encouraging himself—"Don't worry, things will be ok, Jimmy"—and now I understood why.

Still he remained Vincent to me. Whatever I called him, I guess if I had genuinely thought I was done with him, I would have used the letter from Adrienne as an opportunity to send her the diaries. But I wasn't done. Vincent made me laugh, he made me angry, he let me understand a world I didn't know. But most of all, I think I stuck with him because of his dreams. He never described them in much more than a sentence, but they were sensuous, dramatic, and imaginative—filled with trapeze artists, detectives, tropical islands, theaters where he was watching a play he was in, hotels in Spain, churches, and even, on occasion, me. It meant there was more to him than the frequently wooden words on the pages I was reading.

If there was something in his dreams that entranced me, it was his recurring interest in living somewhere other than daily life. He wanted to remove himself from daily life and live it (not act it but live it) in some other medium: a book or a movie, as if either one could be an arena for life itself. "Dreamt that I was in a mystery novel," he wrote one morning on awakening. "Hero went into a secret passageway. The heroine wanted me to go follow him. Came upon a passage where you had to crawl through. I was afraid someone would pull me through from the other side. Hated getting up." Another time, he was in an *I Love Lucy* skit that was being filmed in Chinatown. Once he was even in a computer video game with wizards, hazards, villains, and quests. No medium with a plot escaped his fancy, and yet, oddly, as a diarist he never rendered his life as a story.

I began to understand what Vincent must have wanted from me: it wasn't an edited or annotated volume of his diaries, which I could have helped his family do through a vanity press. He wanted me to make him a story—make a story into him, make him into a story—where he could live forever after.

At least that's what Vincent the dreamer wanted. Vincent awake was another matter. We had been together for three years now, yet I was nowhere near being able to reconcile the cautious, concrete, and constricted man in these diary pages with the bold and open man who'd left his diaries to an English teacher he hadn't laid eyes on for a quarter of a century. However much he wanted to be known, he also wanted not to be known at all. Would he ever clarify himself? He certainly wouldn't if I stopped reading now.

Besides, Vincent had already entered almost as much

into my life as I had entered into his. We were rather like two people on the verge of living together. The carton holding his diaries was now on the floor right beside my desk. My radio was now permanently on top of the carton because the reception was better there than anywhere else in the room. I'd had that radio for years and the reception had never been this good. I took it as a small if inadvertent gift from him. Meanwhile I cleared off a whole shelf on one of the bookcases in my study and lined up all his diaries on it.

Small bits of Vincent's life migrated into my own, piece by piece. One night, I opened the novel on my night table, and was astounded to discover that I'd stuck in Vincent's ticket stub to a Van Cliburn concert as a bookmark. Who's been sleeping in *my* bed? On a visceral level I felt the way Vincent did the first time Ronny came for dinner and slept in his bed. I heard myself make an odd sound, something between a bleat and a gasp.

"What's the matter?" Reamy asked.

I explained. "But I'll get over it," I told him. And I did.

Another time, I was a dollar short when the pizza delivery boy came. Neither of my sons had a dollar and Reamy wasn't home. Then I remembered that Vincent had stuck a dollar bill somewhere in 1990 and so I borrowed it. The next afternoon, I paid him back, too. And once, when I revisited 1986, I found in Vincent's diary a medical insurance claim of Reamy's I'd been searching for madly. I didn't like that. It made my stomach drop.

I didn't think about Vincent all the time, but there was no doubt something had happened. Vincent had become important to me. He had taken up residence in the part of my mind inhabited only by the most significant people in my life, the ones whose birthdays and blood types I know as well as I know my own. And even when I wasn't consciously thinking about him, any daily event could bring him to mind. He was never more than a thought away. Once, in my car heading for the college, I listened to a caller to a consumer advice program ask the host what her son could do so the garbage trucks wouldn't wake him up every morning. "Don't do anything," said the host, "he'll get used to it and he'll sleep right through it."

"Not true!" I said out loud. It didn't make for vivid reading, but year after year, Vincent's first entry for the day was often a complaint about being awakened at dawn by the garbage truck.

By the beginning of 1988, Vincent wasn't sleeping very well during the rest of the night either. The getting-to-know-you part of our relationship was over and hard times were upon us.

"I am worried about purple blotches on my foot & arm," he wrote. Vincent didn't say it out loud, but I knew he knew that purple blotches were a symptom of Kaposi's sarcoma, or KS as it came to be called. Long long ago, before anyone knew about AIDS as such, I'd sat in my kitchen one morning over coffee reading an article in the *New York Times* about the mysterious outbreak of this rare cancer known as Kaposi's sarcoma among gay men in San Francisco. As a lifelong hypochondriac, I had immediately started scanning my own body looking for purple blotches myself.

I'd been with Vincent through a few previous skin eruptions that had sent him rushing to the doctor in a panic. Once it had been poison oak, another time ringworm, and another time, crabs. But this time he was so worried, he was immobilized. "I am so tense. About being alone. And dying. God help us." He dreamt he had been cast in a play whose lines he did not know. "I was sobbing," he wrote.

On April 27, he finally made a doctor's appointment to be tested a week and a half hence, in early May. "I must know," he wrote.

Me, too, I thought. I had decided to live his days along with him one at a time, and though I knew how the diaries would end, I was now alongside him in his present, in for the long haul, as blind to the next day as he was. I knew what would happen, but I didn't know when. Part of my promise to myself was that I wouldn't skip ahead. It would give me a distance and a detachment I both wanted and didn't want.

But now I was worried, too, and for a reason that Vincent didn't even suspect, though he had unwittingly told me.

On April 19, a week before he actually made the decision to go get himself tested, he'd gone to his dentist. "Of course cleaning was painful," he wrote. "No cavities. But film (?) on tongue. Wants to see me [in] 4 more months."

My heart stumbled when I read that. When my son Gabe was two months old, he, too, had had a film on his tongue—in Vincent-time, this was during the week Ronny was admitted to the hospital, in January 1986. Gabriel's pediatrician diagnosed it as thrush, or candidiasis, a yeast infection of the mouth. Because we both had to go on medications, I had to stop nursing him. Thrush in itself was not dangerous, but by 1980, physicians (and presumably dentists) were quite aware that it was one of the earliest signs of an imperiled immune system.

When Vincent's dentist looked into his mouth, he had to have figured something was wrong immediately, although he kept it to himself. But that must have been why he wanted to see Vincent in only four months. Clearly he was in the loop: when Vincent had last visited, in December 1987, he had noticed the dentist had a new getup. We're used to dentists who look like welders now, but this was new to Vincent. "He wore a mask and gloves," he wrote. "Very strange."

When early May came, Vincent changed his mind about getting himself tested. "Almost forgot—canceled Doctor's appointment," he wrote offhandedly on the fifth. What? I literally gasped! I wanted to reach through the page and shake him! How could he cancel!? And how could he "almost forget" to mention it? No explanations were forthcoming. I found it maddening when Vincent turned opaque on me like this.

But trouble was swirling around him, much more than he could deal with. For one, Joey and Vincent were speaking every day by phone because Joey wasn't well either. Vincent, as moody as he'd been in high school, counted on his outgoing and outrageous friend to make him laugh.

Vincent had never mentioned that Joey was HIV positive, but for the first time it was clear to me that he was. "Joey is upset because his T-cells are down," wrote Vincent in May. "May have to start taking medication." AZT. Later I learned that Joey had actually gone to be tested that January, against the advice of practically everyone he knew, including Vincent. (Vincent himself, in the throes of terror, had gone to the Department of Health —just a number, no names necessary—and gotten himself tested a year earlier, according to Joey, whom I spoke with much much later. But to Vincent, the terror of knowing was greater than the terror of not knowing. He never called for the results.)

May 22, 1988, was the second anniversary of Ronny's death. Vincent remembered it and commented on it. He was clearly in a frightened torpor, but luckily for him, Joey's own health concerns somehow pushed him to act in Vincent's behalf. He was out of patience with sitting by and watching Vincent do nothing.

So he had begun peppering Vincent with phone calls, nagging him to get himself tested. In June, Vincent agreed. He made an appointment for July 1.

This time, though he woke up with dread and walked through the day with dread, he kept it. "Left work at 3:30 P.M." At work his closest friend was Sharon. She was the boss's wife and someone who could make Vincent laugh out loud. She drove him to Dr. Raszyl's and dropped him off. "We joked about Dr. Razzle Dazzle. Went to wrong building. Found right place. After 20 minutes doctor showed up. Did not live up to his name. Asked me a bunch of questions. Told him about purple spots. Diagnosed them KS. I have fuckin' AIDS. Went into shock. Tried to console me. Went to [supermarket]. Wrote bad check. Called Joey. Not home. Joey called. I spilled my guts. Told him to tell no one."

Later I learned that a transcript of that phone conversation existed, although I never really knew whether it was a recorded account that Vincent had transcribed or an imaginative dialogue based on the real conversation.

Joey: Vincent, pick up the phone. I know you're there, Vincent.

Vincent: What do you want, Joey?

Joey: Is everything all right?

Vincent: No.

Joey: What happened?

Vincent: I don't want to talk about it.

Joey: Where have you been?

Vincent: In bed, under the covers, watching cartoons. I just don't want to think.

Joey: What did the doctor say?

Vincent: He got the results back from my blood test. I'm positive. Don't tell anybody.

Joey: I won't. Well, you figured. But what was your first reaction when he told you?

Vincent: Suicide.

Joey: We have to get you into therapy.

Vincent: That's what the doctor said. I just don't want to be in a Who's Afraid of Virginia Woolf situation.

Joey: They're not like that, they're very supportive.

Vincent: Great! That's what I need, pity.

Joey: Give it a chance. What else did he say?

Vincent: He took more blood. God I hate needles. Some test with letters and numbers.

Joey: P24?

Vincent: Yeah, I think so. He wants me to start taking AZT while I'm still strong enough to deal with it. My T-cell count is barely borderline passable.

Joey: Well, then get a second opinion.

Vincent: I blame this all on Ronald Reagan. It took the man more than four years to even say the fuckin' word. The man is dangerous.

Joey: When do you see the doctor again?

Vincent: Next week. I'm supposed to call him Wednesday for the results of my tests. Joey, I'm scared.

Joey: I know but you've got to be strong.

Vincent: I can't sleep. The doctor gave me a prescription for sleeping pills.

Joey: Great, you're thinking about suicide and he gives you sleeping pills.

Vincent: Don't you know people who talk about suicide never do it.

Joey: You better not.

Vincent: I won't.

Joey: When you go home for Christmas are you going to tell your family?

Vincent: No way. Why worry them? They can't do anything.

Joey: I think you should.

Vincent: I think you should mind your own business.

Joey: It's better to prepare them now. You can tell them in person.

Vincent: This may be the last time I see them while I'm still healthy.

Joey: Don't say that. You can't give up. You have to have a more positive attitude.

Vincent: I saw what it did to Ronny. I don't want to be like that. I'm too vain.

Joey: Ronny shot up, Vincent. It affects everyone differently. They also know more about the disease than when Ronny had it. You have to hang in there.

Vincent: I just want to live to the turn of the century.

Joey: You're going to live way past that. We're going to be old maids together. Now get out of bed. Take a shower. And let's do a movie. Something funny.

Vincent: Not now. I don't feel like one.

Joey: Well you don't look like one. Okay, I understand. But we have to get you into a group.

Vincent: Anything you say, Martha.

Joey: Shut up, George.

Vincent: Joey, thank you.

Joey: For what?

Vincent: You know.

Joey: I know.

Vincent: I'm gonna go. I want to wallow in self-pity for a while.

Joey: I understand. I'll talk to you later.

Vincent's perspective on his own life now changed radically and suddenly: he knew his future was limited, and his zeal, or maybe it was his need, to make a fuller permanent record of his daily life intensified. Only hours after his diagnosis, he wrote in more detail than usual about his experience going to Dr. Raszyl's with Sharon, and soon after, his conversation with Joey.

Joey was there for Vincent all summer just as he had been in that first late afternoon phone call. He took Vincent shopping, he invited Vincent to stay at his house when Vincent got afraid, he took Vincent to the movies, he came up with a therapist's name, he tried to make Vincent laugh, he got Vincent to take vitamins. Sometime that summer, in appreciation, Vincent found just the right gift for Joey: the soundtrack to *Stand By Me*.

Joey kept Vincent's secret throughout the rest of the

spring and early summer, but by late July, Joey was feeling the burden of the secret keeper. He and Vincent were coming east together in August. Joey already knew Angela, Adrienne, and Sandra. Now he was going to meet Vincent's parents as well, and he didn't want to lie to them in his silence. He wanted Vincent to tell his parents that he was HIV positive.

Vincent refused. No way!

A few weeks later, Joey's urging turned to nagging. Bluntly, Joey finally told Vincent that he was worried that if Vincent died, he, Joey, would have to be the one to tell Vincent's parents. He didn't want Vincent's family to be unprepared. He didn't want to deliver such shocking news. The two argued, but Vincent would not change his mind.

Vincent was used to keeping his parents out of his life. In his diary, he usually referred to them distantly as "Mother and Father," but his sisters were another matter. Vincent had always been extremely close to "the girls," and they were to him as well. But he didn't want to tell them either because he didn't want to worry them, and just as much to the point, he didn't want them to nag him.

August came, and Vincent and Joey went east, and Joey kept his promise and said not a word. On the last day of his visit to his family in the east, just before he left for the airport, Vincent called Angela at work to say good-bye. Then he got in the car with Angela's boyfriend, Richie, who was driving him to JFK. At the terminal, Vincent got out of the car, and walked to the back of the car, expecting Richie to pop the trunk so he could get his baggage. But to his astonishment, Richie drove off. "My luggage still in trunk," Vincent later wrote. "Freaked out. No jacket. Luckily I had keys & plane tickets. [But] AZT, checks, clothes, candy for office and DIARY in suitcase. So upset."

Four days after Vincent flew back to San Francisco, Angela called.

She knew.

"She read my diary (by mistake of course). I was upset. She was upset. 'Do I need anything? Money?' Told her to come to SF for Christmas. Conversation was awkward, guarded. Agreed not to tell mother & father . . . After we hung up could not stop thinking about it. Sort of upset that she read it, but felt sorry that she had to find out this way."

Upset, upset, upset, sorry. But not angry that Angela had read his diary. I wondered—had Vincent somehow engineered this meeting between Angela and his diary? He not only brought his diary with him wherever he went, but he often paraded it about like a very small dog. But as couples sometimes have a division of labor between them in relation to the outside world, so occasionally did Vincent and his diary. He counted on those he knew to read his diary, and when they did, it was his emissary, his messenger, his explicator, and on occasion, it played bad cop to his good cop.

Once, when he was a guest at someone's house, he complained to his diary about how his host exercised complete control over the TV remote, making Vincent "a slave to his awful taste." Then he turned reflective. "And you wonder why people are upset when they read your diary?"

The most elaborate ménage à trois commenced one winter when Vincent had his old friend Craig as a houseguest. Craig, who I remembered as a guest at Vincent's Christmas dinner party several years earlier, had returned to San Francisco after a few years in New York as a runway model, and told Vincent he would only be staying "a few days" till he found his own apartment. They were no longer even casual sexual partners, as they once had been, but given Vincent's HIV-positive status, I waited to see how Vincent would handle telling Craig, but whatever he said, he didn't confide in his diary.

Meanwhile, the days turned into weeks and the weeks turned into months, and Vincent was incapable of telling Craig to make other arrangements. But day after day, he seethed and muttered to his diary. "Craig sleeps too late

. . . Craig primps too much . . . Craig has an ugly body." Knowing that Vincent was given to parading his diary, I suspected that Craig quickly became an avid daily reader. More to the point, I knew Vincent well enough to believe that he knew Craig was reading his diary, and deliberately used the diary as a weapon, hoping the bullets that came out of his pen would ricochet off the page and hit Craig right between his inquiring and intrusive eyes.

The day Craig moved out, he took his revenge. He opened up Vincent's diary for the last time, and then he committed the ultimate intrusion. In a sprawling script, he wrote two sentences in Vincent's diary that covered half a page. "In your note to me this morning, Vincent, you mentioned strength and support from your friends would see you through the days ahead. I'm so happy I'm not a part of that group." He signed it "Craig!!!" Astoundingly, Vincent ignored it entirely, treating it as if it weren't even there. And he never mentioned Craig again.

ONE DAY WHILE IN the middle of reading about Craig's stay, I drove to Brooklyn to visit my mother, and as we sat in her kitchen having sandwiches and coffee, she asked me what I was working on. I told her about Vincent and his diaries and Craig and about how I'd been thinking about what it means to read someone else's diary or to let someone read yours.

"That reminds me," she said. "Once when I was young,

I was dating someone named Gordon. He was very handsome, and I was wild about him. We were studying acting in a repertory company together." The best memories of her life were from the time in her twenties when she had been an actress. Way-off Broadway, she'd done Thornton Wilder and Clifford Odets. Once, on Broadway, she'd starred in August Strindberg's *Bridal Crown* for all of its three-day run.

"Every night after rehearsal," she told me, "Gordon would take me home by subway from the acting studio in Manhattan to Brooklyn. Then he would get back on the subway and return to the apartment in the Village he shared with Alex, another member of the company. But the relationship with Gordon didn't seem to be going anywhere. He never kissed me. Then one day he showed me his diary. There was a passage which praised me to the skies and then it said, 'I wish it were truly possible for me to love her.'"

Fifty years later, and she still remembered the line verbatim, and repeated it again. "I wish it were truly possible for me to love her."

"What did you think was going on?"

"I was young and very naive. I didn't understand at all. I told the line to my best friend, Dorothy, and asked her what she thought he meant. 'Oh, Aurora,' Dorothy said, 'He's trying to tell you he's a homo.'"

In the months following Vincent's diagnosis, he

began to adjust to a future he now understood was limited. At his best, he struck a balance between fatalism and humor, and nowhere was this more apparent than in a small but telling incident at work. For some time, Vincent had kept an ant farm in his cubicle near his desk. Though the space was entirely his, it had no door and only rib-high walls on three sides. Anyone passing by could readily see anything on his desk or on any other surface in his space. Like all ant farms, Vincent's had gone from thriving to moribund, but he kept it on display all the same. One morning, he arrived to find a note in his box from his boss letting him know (somewhat apologetically) that an unnamed coworker had complained about his visible ant cemetery. Could he please, asked his boss, move it to some place less visible?

Well, of course there wasn't any place less visible, and that meant Vincent's ant farm had to go. He guessed immediately who the complainer was and referred to her acidly as "Roach Lady" in his diary that day. Nevertheless the memo he sent her the next day was good-natured. "When those critters were alive they were an inspiration to us all to work harder for mere crumbs, against all odds. Real morale boosters. But now that they have gone to that big ant farm in the sky, their remnants are not only a means of my self-expression, but a reminder to us all that we are not permanent and can easily be replaced."

Meanwhile, he looked for other boosters in his life. Joey, his sisters, and the dailiness of his job were his "support system," he told himself. He fell asleep listening to arias because they soothed him, and more than once woke up singing Madonna's "Like a Prayer." He exercised regularly at the gym. He had long worked out with weights and was very proud of his compact and muscular body.

But when he'd developed his first KS lesion, his shorts and tank tops went into his dresser drawer and stayed there. From then on, to the gym he wore sweatpants and long-sleeved shirts. By night, in dreams worthy of Hawthorne, his lesions became marks of shame, marks of sin, marks of isolation. In one dream (of several dozen on the theme) he was sexually approached by Michael Jordan, but he resisted Michael's entreaties for only one reason: he didn't want Michael to see the lesions on his back.

Vincent also made many fruitless efforts to give up pot. March 28, 1989, was one of many mornings he wrote about smoking pot the very first thing. As I was reading the entry, a fortune cookie fortune fluttered down from his diary page and onto my lap. "There is yet time enough for you to take a different path," it said.

The living are the flat ones.
You might expect the dead to shrink to two dimensions,

but no, they thicken, put on bulk and plumpness
until they seem more solid than the skinny
shapes of the living.

RACHEL HADAS
"In the Grove"

———◦◦◦———

SOMETHING WAS HAPPENING HERE.

My feelings were coming in, not the way momentarily delayed pain comes to a hammered finger, which is what I had expected, but more the way color comes into a tomato. What happened was quietly astounding to me. When people I knew died, I had been unable to resurrect them internally—never fully and not even partially for a long time.

But now a dead man I had never really known had quickened in me—no wooden Pinocchio, and not even the fourteen year old I had known so long ago, but someone else, someone new, a real live man. It startled me, suggesting new possibilities: a door connecting the two realms instead of the lead wall separating the living from the dead.

I liked Vincent, shortcomings and all. I also knew how he thought, what he liked, what he didn't like. I could even predict how he was going to react to something. But how had this happened? Raising the dead was not something I could will, or anyone could will. I did know, though, that I had not done it alone. Through his words, Vincent had collaborated with me in his own resurrection, exactly as he had intended. And now he and I were in conversation.

I knew, however, that there was limited time and a finite number of pages between today and the day when the conversation would stop. What if without him, I couldn't carry on the conversation with him?

On his side of the diary page, it was the chilly end of 1990. On my side, it was now a hot and humid August in 1995. Maybe because I knew Vincent's diaries to be such seasoned travelers, I put a few aside to take with me as we packed up for a few weeks' vacation in Cape Cod.

I was not going away easily, and I would not have gone at all had I not found Joan Morris, a neighborhood woman who would look in on my mother regularly. Fiercely independent, my mother was not happy when Joan, my sister, and I all met at my mother's house for the first time, and she had nothing pleasant to say when

I called later to ask how their first hours together had gone after my sister and I left.

"I don't need anyone to help me," she said stonily.

"Let's talk about it next time I come for lunch."

"You can bring your own lunch."

At my next visit, while making sandwiches for both of us, my mother returned to the subject of her vanishing memory. "By tomorrow I probably won't be sure if you visited today or last week or not at all. Sometimes I know an event has occurred, but I don't know how recently. If we were talking about sight, I'd say my depth perception was off."

"How can you remember what it is that you can't remember?"

She screwed the cap on the mayonnaise. "I don't know. Memory is strange that way. Sometimes I see a silhouette of experience, sometimes it's just a toe sticking through the sand, and I know if I dig and am patient, I can get the whole thing back." She shrugged. "And sometimes there isn't anything at all."

"Well, I'll remind you to write today down in your diary."

"How do you know about my diary?" she asked evenly.

"You always leave it out on the kitchen counter. It's right there," I said pointing to the other end of the counter where she stood. "Last time I was here, I asked you if I could look at it, and you said OK."

I had begun to look at her diary fairly regularly so I could see how she was doing. She didn't seem to mind. Or maybe it was just that she didn't remember for long enough to really brood about it. In spite of my entreaties, she was still driving her 1972 VW Beetle, and in her diary she now listed her travels. "Went to Rock Bottom for cigarettes," or "Went to Waldbaum's." Even "Elizabeth called," or "Ginny visited." Like Vincent, but for different reasons, my mother had become a cataloger.

"I used to write to ventilate, mostly about your father," she said, bringing the sandwiches to the table, and sitting down. "But I guess I write in my diary now so that I'll have proof that whatever-it-is happened at all. But when I read back over it," she explained, "it doesn't trigger a memory."

She shook her head. "I just never thought it would be my mind," she said quietly, more to herself than to me.

Even ancient memories firmly within my mother's grasp weren't always what they had been. Some that had once been pleasurable turned rancid on her; on the other hand, a few bitter ones lost their edge. Her marriage to my father, dead for almost twenty-five years, had now improved considerably. When memories about him occurred to her they were likely to be about the time he put on his fishing hip boots and climbed into the Dumpster near the A & P to get discarded vegetables, which he brought back in his net for my sister's horse, or the time he caught a horseshoe crab and tried to steam it with garlic, or the time he painted half the bathtub Day-Glo orange. I was struck again with how liquid memory could be, not solid or fixed. And now, with so many of my mother's recent experiences inscribed in invisible ink, she didn't even have the experiences she *did* have.

My mother's eroded memory also upset me selfishly. Her changing and vanished past affected what had been *our* past. We no longer stood on the same mountain of shared experiences, and I could feel it, just as Kevin McCarthy felt it in *Invasion of the Body Snatchers*. But that title was wrong. What was snatched wasn't her body, but something more ineffable.

Together Vincent and my mother, one gone and the other going, were enabling me to think about memory freshly, and about exactly what kind of preservation had eluded me in the face of death or departure or even alteration. It was not that my experiences disappeared on me but that devastating deaths and losses pressed on my memories like a rock slab, draining them of color and substance till they became like blanched leaves under a rock.

At the Cape, amidst worried calls to my mother as

well as pleasurable afternoons on the dune-backed beaches with my family and our friends, I spent some time with Vincent and his diaries. His "support system" was weakening now. Work was becoming stressful. He was thinking of leaving his job altogether and going on disability. Also, for reasons Vincent never explained, he and Joey had had a falling out. For several months, they didn't see each other at all, and Vincent didn't so much as mention Joey's name. Then they formally ended their friendship, returning each other's house keys. Meanwhile, Angela wanted Vincent to move to Brooklyn, so he could live closer to her. No way, he wrote. He wanted to stay in his apartment. He wanted to be left alone.

This is not what I would have wanted at all. Long ago, I'd read about contact species (like walruses), which flop all over each other, and noncontact species (like birds), which need their own space. I was definitely a walrus, and never more so than when I was scared or in trouble. For most of my life, I'd also believed that birds were really walruses who were lying.

But now my gaze was fixed on the daily life of a bird who had no reason to lie, and I found it oddly persuasive, even soothing. I had more access to Vincent and his life as he lived it than I'd ever had to anyone in my entire life. My mother was another bird, and now, day by day, here was Vincent, a dead man, explaining the ways of birds to me in a way that made sense, teaching me something I didn't know. I was grateful to him.

He really didn't want to answer the phone when it rang. And never had. He really didn't want to travel with anyone, and often enough, he didn't want to go through with the dinner plans he'd made with Carol or Joey or Sharon. He wasn't just saying it, he meant it. Same with my mother, who sometimes took the phone off the hook because she didn't want to be bothered, never wanted to go anywhere, and didn't want to meet anyone she didn't already know. What would have struck me as an unendurable solitary confinement seemed to Vincent—and perhaps to my mother—often a pleasant-enough solitude. Reading Vincent's diaries was like taking a crash course in Otherness: understanding differences between people in realms I hadn't even thought of as realms, learning that someone else wasn't just Me Manqué.

Vincent had his first dream about me, too, during this period of adjustment, but I was no help. I was his teacher, and I was giving a test on a book he hadn't read. He was scared.

On my last night in Cape Cod, I had a dream of my own: Vincent and I are riding up and down an elevator in an apartment building, which soon turns into a hospital. He is Vincent the grown man, not Vincent the child. In the dream he is terribly pale and looks very

weak. His breathing is labored. We are in the elevator together, going from one floor to another, up and down
and up. We are looking for the right floor, though what
makes it the right floor or what we'll find there, I don't
know. Does Vincent know? He's not saying. I'm disori-
ented, I sense danger.

Then suddenly Vincent has next year's red diary in his
hands. In my dream, hospitals give out diaries to patients
the way dentists give out toothbrushes or dental floss.
Something to cleanse, to maintain well-being. Or maybe
I have gotten the diary for him? I'm not sure. Anyhow,
Vincent is happy. He is holding the red diary.

After a while, he begins to cough and cough, the diary
pressed to his chest, his skin purpling and crumpling
alarmingly with the exertion. Finally, he coughs so hard
that he splatters blood all over everything—his shirt, the
walls, my shirt, my fingers and hands. "I have blood
on my hands" runs the thought through my dreaming
mind.

I look at my bloody hands, thinking if he's coughing
blood, he will not be able to stay with us, my family and
me, any longer. His blood is lethal. We have two sons.
Reamy will have to tell Vincent to leave. Vincent reads
my thoughts somehow and lunges at me in rage. I scream
so loudly I wake myself up. I also wake up Reamy, Paul,
Gabriel, and undoubtedly a good many others in the cot-

tages nearby. I have never screamed myself awake from a dream before.

In the dark in an unfamiliar house, we reassure our boys and wait till their breathing is even again. In our own bed, Reamy, another walrus, inches closer and we fall asleep. In my green Vincent notebook, I write, "Has my home turned into a hospital under the burden of these red diaries?" And just whose red diaries am I thinking of anyhow? Wedged between two diarists, Vincent and my mother, I fear I have not quite been a member of my family's daily world for quite some time. They don't like it and neither do I.

The next morning under a bright Cape Cod sun, sitting outside my cottage on an Adirondack chair amidst the pungent smell of dry pine needles, I turn the page to read the next day's entry in Vincent's diary. I see that the previous night, Vincent, too, has dreamt about being stuck in an elevator. I have no explanation.

ON SATURDAY, NOVEMBER 7, 1992, a few days after Bill Clinton defeated George Bush in the presidential election (to Vincent's relief, and mine, too), Vincent's class at New Utrecht High School had its twenty-year reunion, and as we approached that date, I read with special anticipation and some uncertainty.

Vincent knew about the reunion long in advance, although he wasn't sure he wanted to go. On the other hand, since he wasn't sure he didn't, he kept his options open. He was planning to travel around Europe in the fall, so when he made his travel arrangements, he booked a flight back on November 4, three days before the reunion. He wanted to visit Angela and Adrienne anyway.

Michael Musto, the gossip columnist, loomed large in Vincent's deliberations. Musto had been in Vincent's graduating class, and Vincent was curious to see whether he would show up. If there was anyone's life Vincent coveted, it was Musto's. Over the years, Vincent mentioned every time he saw Michael Musto on TV or came across his byline. He was the "star" Vincent had always wished he could be.

By Friday, November 6, the day before the reunion, Vincent was still vacillating, and I was impatient with him, annoyed that his case of nerves might make me miss the reunion as well. Would he go? Because I had decided to live his days alongside him, I had not looked ahead. On Saturday morning, he went shopping, hoping to find something that would bolster his courage and tip the balance. At an A & S sale, he found a sports jacket (38R) he liked for ninety dollars. Back at his parents', he tried the jacket on again in front of the mirror.

"Although I looked good, I did not want to go to reunion," he wrote. "Did not leave until 7:30 P.M." The re-union was to be held at a local nightclub, and a relative who was a glazier gave Vincent a lift in his truck. "Felt a little uneasy watching women enter Hollywood Terrace wearing minks as I exit from Glass Truck."

His uneasiness did not last. He circled the hall, warily at first, but gathering courage as he spotted one familiar face after another. "I knew practically everyone! Never knew how popular I was in school," he wrote, reveling in the recollection. "So happy to see most of the kids."

The next day he was still in high spirits. "Could not stop talking about reunion." No Michael Musto, though. "Did not want to expose us to the paparazzi. GMAB."

At home after the reunion, he made a list of all the classmates he knew, a rich man counting up his pieces of gold. "Chris, Joanne, Amy (looked great), John, Vinny (bald), David (still married), John captain football (still gorgeous), Marlene, Mary. Told Michelle (she had her nose fixed) that I had a crush on her," and more.

As he listed each name, I felt as if I were looking over his shoulder, caught up in his excitement because maybe I would know someone, too. And finally I did—Freddy Murphy, the bespectacled boy who'd sat right in front of Vincent, turned up, alive, well, and still living in Ben-sonhurst. This wasn't just a cameo appearance but his reentry into Vincent's life. Vincent was sure Freddy was gay, but equally sure Freddy had never acted on it. He was unmarried and still living with his mother and father in Bensonhurst, in the house he'd grown up in, still sleeping in the single bed he'd always slept in—to Vincent, a cramped thin bed in a cramped thin life. Though Vincent must have envied Freddy's health, in some unvoiced but unmistakable way, he pitied Freddy's constriction. Freddy was the road not taken. At this moment of assessment, Vincent found he had no regrets.

The New Utrecht High School reunion was an occasion of enormous significance for Vincent, a real reunion. What Vincent had always needed above all else was someone to watch over him, to see him; someone who would keep him in mind. There were never enough people like that in his life, especially in his community now so barbarously pruned by AIDS.

In a few months, he would be leaving work and a nest of colleagues whom he'd known for ten years. But the New Utrecht reunion brought many people back into Vincent's psychic life. For the rest of his days, they would provide his most soothing and generous audience, awake and in dreams. Vincent and Freddy wrote and phoned each other, and eventually Vincent sent Freddy a copy of Armistead Maupin's *Tales of the City* because it had affected him so deeply. "Made me miss the past," he wrote in his diary. "There are so many hidden secrets only San

Franciscans would understand. I truly love living in S.F. Wish I can continue."

⚬⚬⚬

As 1993 BEGAN, Vincent counted the days till he could leave his job, and the unpleasant world of ringing alarm clocks, crowded buses, greasy muffins, and office feuds. On April 1, Vincent celebrated his last day as a commercial insurance underwriter at Eckert & Hauser. "First day of disability," he exulted the next morning. "No more work."

But Vincent also knew he was entering an unmapped limbo with its own perils. Tucked into his diary that day was a mock Monopoly card, the kind you pick up when you land on Community Chest. "Get Out of Purgatory Free . . . this card may be kept until needed." It showed a frog with wings and a halo flying out of a cage.

Whatever else work was for Vincent, it was a nest, warm and full. Without it, Vincent was out on a bare limb, left to face the frailty of his ties to other people. His days were empty and uneventful, and Vincent was often crestfallen. At such moments, he wished for someone to hold him and cuddle with him. But there had never been anyone like that in his life, and there wasn't now either. "I'll be alone the rest of my life," he wrote mournfully. Then, he turned on himself. "Get a pet."

By now Vincent had either given up—or given up

on—the bars, another world where he had a string of acquaintances. He had often prided himself on being a "star" at such places. But now, with disfiguring red lesions on his arms and legs and torso, he feared rejection by anyone who might see his body. And so he drifted back to the baths with their dim lights. Most baths were now banned in San Francisco as hotbeds of contagion, so he had to take public transportation all the way to Berkeley to get to Steamworks, his bath of choice.

Now that he was HIV positive, sex was a lot more complicated, or should have been. In principle, Vincent believed his partners were entitled to know he was HIV positive, but he often stalled in the telling. The Ecstasy or acid he often took before his forays did not enhance his candor.

One Sunday, Vincent met a man named Ken and they spent a Rabelaisian afternoon together. The uncensored flow of his thoughts that night reveal the messy mixture of guilt and desire he felt.

> He was there from the night before w/his lover. Ken was cute . . . Lover was creepy. We played till 5:00. Place filled with pretty men. But I wasn't interested. We exchanged #s. Left by 6:00 P.M. Dined @ Burger King. Home by 8:00 P.M. Ken called. Let machine pick it up.

Must tell him that I am positive. I hate it.
Dreamt that [my sister] Sandra & I were trying
to figure out who was killed in the cellar &
every time we went down there we left our
fingerprints on the bloody murder weapon &
were chased. Definitely not enough sleep. Felt
effects of acid yesterday. Of course I kept
thinking about Ken.

The next day, Monday, he had more knotted and
gnarled thoughts about Ken. "Was hoping and dreading
Ken calling. I know he will break your heart. You gotta
be honest. Need more sleeping pills. Stopped taking anti-
depressants."

Tuesday, more of the same.

Occasionally fantasized over Ken. Know it
won't work out . . . Called Eddy Cavello. His
friend Joseph tried to kill himself by slashing his
wrists. Poor poor Eddy. Sleeping pill still has
not kicked in. Took injection. . . . I still want to
see Ken again. He never called.

Thursday, Ken left a message, and Vincent called back
and left one in return. When he hadn't heard from Ken
by Friday, he called again.

Lover answered. Very awkward. Hate playing the other woman. Ken told me he'd call me back. Tried finding a shrink. Did laundry & [groceries]. Picked up more drugs. Took a nap. Ken called. I really like him. But must tell him I'm positive. Plan on getting together Sunday for brunch.

Finally Sunday came.

Ken left two messages. Coming over between 11:30 and noon . . . Must tell him I'm positive or else. . . . Ken arrived before noon. Brought beautiful flowers. We started off heavy petting. Eventually moved it into the bedroom. Hid my scars. Never told him about being positive.

Tuesday, he mentioned Ken again. "Moved Ken's flowers to my bedroom so that I can think about him."

Wednesday: "Ken never called. . . . His flowers still smell."

Thursday: "Ken never called. Flowers are dying."

Throughout the week, Vincent's entire focus was on a phone that didn't ring. A week later, when Ken still hadn't called, Vincent sank into the dank lonely pit I'd seen him in before. "No one will ever love me again. Ken my last hope." In his diary, the Sunday of the brunch became the final resting place for a single translucent pink petal from Ken's bouquet. That's where Vincent placed it, and that's where I found it. But he never did tell Ken or Ken's lover that he was HIV positive. Months later, he saw Ken in the company of another man at Steamworks. I assume he didn't tell either one of them.

On July 21, without any more emotion than usual, Vincent wrote, "Dreamt that Tim Eustace (the man in Florida who contaminated me) was in my house seducing & manipulating me. They brought in a mattress. I told him to remove it." Then, without further comment, he was on to another dream.

I wanted to yank those lines apart! Vincent knew who had infected him with AIDS? Really? In the five years since he'd tested positive, he'd picked up a pen and opened his diary nearly two thousand times, but not once had he ruminated about how or where or from whom he might have contracted his illness, and never had he said he knew. Now, here was this casual allusion to Tim Eustace —within parentheses, no less. I was shocked that this was not a new thought to him. And who was Tim? I was struck by how little Vincent actually confided in his diary.

As to his notion that he knew who had infected him, was such knowledge even possible? I called my friend

Steve who had lived in San Francisco for the previous twenty years. He and I had gone to high school together, and he had been a significant force in my intellectual life. Steve and I had worked together as editors on the school paper. The printer was on Barrow Street in Greenwich Village, and after the paper was put to bed, we prowled Greenwich Village bookstores together. It was Steve who had first introduced me to the *New Yorker,* Dalton Trumbo, Ayn Rand, and films with subtitles. He had known then, and told me then, that he was gay, though he didn't want to be.

After high school, with each of us in college on opposite sides of the country, we had drifted apart. I knew he had married briefly and unsuccessfully, and I had heard that after his marriage, he had moved to San Francisco (at just about the time Vincent had). In the intervening decades, I had made several efforts to find him. When I couldn't, I feared he might have died of AIDS. Somehow, though, he had found me, and one day wrote to say he was alive and well and still living in San Francisco.

So when I got Steve on the phone that day I asked him if the kind of knowledge Vincent claimed to have was possible.

"It's possible," he said hesitantly, "or at least many people who are HIV positive think it is." Steve himself was not HIV positive, but a few years earlier he had taken care of a former lover who was dying. Subsequently he had become a volunteer grief counselor. The lore, he told me, was that the sexual encounter that actually infected you might be followed by a flurry of flu-like symptoms a week or two or three later. "But you get those symptoms three or four months before you could even show up positive on a blood test. Still, many people feel that at least in hindsight, you have some idea who infected you."

I did vaguely remember that Vincent had been to Florida some years earlier, but I didn't remember anyone named Tim. I went shuffling through my diary on Vincent's diaries and found that Vincent had taken a trip to Florida seven years earlier, in March 1986.

His diary for that year was my least favorite because its pages were the smallest—4" x 6"—and therefore let Vincent be his most elliptical. But I found what I was looking for. About two months before Ronny died, Vincent had spent a week and a half in Florida with Robert, his antique dealer friend who had always made him laugh when they spoke on the phone, and who now lived in Atlanta.

"Made it to Robert's," Vincent had written on his arrival, gear in hand including his diary and camera, which always went with him. "It rained so I stayed indoors, unpacked, unwound, took a shower and exercised.

Sneaked his picture. Rehearsed it prior," whatever that meant. "He looks great, but still drinks too much."

Vincent had needed to get away from Ronny's deterioration at the time, but this vacation was a ten-day lost weekend filled with too much drinking and too much cruising. They left Atlanta almost immediately, taking turns driving through the night and part of the next day until they reached Fort Lauderdale. There, they met two men whom Vincent described as hustlers, and spent a day with them engaged in activities about which, thankfully, Vincent remained elliptical. A day and a half later, apparently without even a full night's sleep between them, they were on the road again, headed for Key West, already known for welcoming gay tourists.

On their first night in Key West, Robert headed straight for the bars and came back drunk a few hours later. The man he brought with him to their hotel room was Tim Eustace. Then, for some unexplained reason, Robert left again, and the apparently omnivorous Tim turned his attention to Vincent. That night and a good part of the next day they were together.

"He accompanies me through the town," Vincent wrote the next day. "I buy him lunch. He wants me to buy him a jacket or a hat. He's a hustler all right. After lunch he comes back to hotel. We take nap. I just can't get rid of him. Robert is absolutely no help. I explain to

Tim that he cannot spend the night. Robert returns drunk & passes out on the bed. Tim & I go out drinking. I pay. I buy a poster for Ronny. Home by 2:00 A.M. I must get rid of him. Finally succeed and Robert returns around 5:30 A.M."

But the next night at 8:30, Robert again walked into the hotel room with Tim Eustace. "I am so mad at Robert," Vincent fumed to his diary. "Now once again I must get rid of him. Eventually I escort him out & of course he 'borrows' $2—for breakfast." Once they'd gotten rid of Tim for good, Vincent and Robert hashed the whole mess out. "I blame him for bringing him into the room in the first place & he blames me for stealing him. By the time we're driving back home, we are once again friends." And that was that. No further mention of Tim.

But I was puzzled. Vincent was persistently (and understandably) preoccupied with his health, so much so that almost anything could strike him as potentially dire. Nevertheless, when he came back from Key West, and for the next month (which I reread just to be sure), there was not a word about a headache or fever or chills. So why, four years after his diagnosis and six years after Key West, was Vincent pointing the finger at Tim? More to the point, given Vincent's risky carelessness, any number of candidates were available as the source of his AIDS, so why the focus on Tim?

I didn't know, and Vincent said nothing more. So I left 1986 and came back to 1993, wending my way through the rest of the summer and the fall. On December 7, with a little more than a year to live and now in daily pain, Vincent returned to the subject of Tim for the last time. In one of the briefest entries in all his journals he wrote:

> Once again did not sleep much. Would fall asleep and wake up w/in ten minutes in pain. I have not slept in 3 days. Never let Dr. Malater inject you w/his medicine. I hate Robert for bringing Tim Eustace into our room; then leaving. But I blame myself for unsafe sex.

Now that he was ill, was he trying to make his past, his present, and what remained of his future coherent? That's when it occurred to me that in one way Tim was different from anyone else in Vincent's battalion of fleeting sexual partners: Since Tim had been with both Vincent and Robert, it may have been that Tim *connected* Vincent to Robert. And his first voiced accusation against Tim came at a time when he was deeply isolated, cut off from the hum of daily life, his future, and his friends. His illness bloomed more poisonously every day, but he could make it less fearsome by rooting it in a familiar and domestic soil. Was it even true? Who knew? And who *could* know? But it was a connection.

By now, I had an established relationship with Vincent, and it was time—beyond time—to meet his sisters in person. I'd spoken with all three of them by phone, and all three had been extremely gracious. Sandra lived in North Carolina now, but Angela and Adrienne and I arranged to meet one night at an Italian restaurant in Bensonhurst, where both women live.

I got there first, sat down on a bench in front of the restaurant, and minutes later saw two attractive women in pastel sundresses crossing the street, walking toward me. I recognized them instantly, just from their physical bearing. Neither one is especially short but both are delicate—with small frames like Vincent's. Angela especially reminded me so strongly of Vincent—the line of her jaw and an intensity in her eyes that I suddenly remembered seeing in his. It was like finding a lost memory. Someone hums a bar of music, and suddenly you remember a whole song you forgot you knew. Seeing them, I knew what Vincent's adult heft must have been like.

It was a long evening. As we sat at the restaurant table, the fourth seat seeming increasingly empty, we traded reminiscences, asked questions, and offered clarifications. They knew most of Vincent's friends, living and dead. Joey, Carol, Sharon, Eddy Cavello, Ronny, and even poor DDD.

"And Joey's still with Jan in Amsterdam," Adrienne told me.

"And DDD?"

He had been incredibly generous when Angela and Sandra came for Vincent's last week, driving anyone anywhere at anytime. "He took Vincent to the hospital that last time."

"And do you know someone named Robert?" I was reluctant to mention Robert at all because I was afraid it would lead to revelations about Vincent that would hurt them. And yet, if I were going to write about Vincent (and tonight's conversation made it clear that they did want me to) I was going to have to write about the man I knew, lesions and all.

"Oh Robert," said Angela. "He's moved back north."

"Back north? I thought Vincent knew him from San Francisco."

"Oh no," said Angela. "He lived out there for a while, but he's from Brooklyn."

"You know him?"

"Oh sure," said Adrienne. "His name is Robert Likowski, and our family and his family are old friends from the neighborhood."

Meanwhile, Angela was going through a pile of photographs she'd brought in a manila envelope to show me, finally handing me a picture of a corpulent man with tight curly black hair and a full beard. In the photo, Robert was holding his hand up as if he didn't want his picture taken. It reminded me of Vincent's comment when he first arrived at Robert's about sneaking his picture. Maybe that was that photograph.

The lighting in the restaurant was soft, so I held the photograph closer to the candle on our table in order to see it more clearly. The man in the photo had sad eyes, and now that I was looking closely, I saw they were sad golden-brown eyes.

"Wait a second," I said, "Were Robert and Vincent friends in high school?"

"Yes," said Adrienne.

And that's when I knew: Robert Likowski was Robby, the quiet boy with the sad golden-brown eyes whom Vincent had brought to my apartment on his one and only visit twenty-five years earlier. So Robby had been gay, too. With that information, I had my first glimpse into that friendship between two fourteen-year-old boys coming to terms with being gay in an inhospitable environment. Did they talk to each other about it? Rue their fate? Fool around with each other?

"We don't know," said Angela looking at Adrienne, who nodded her assent.

"Still, in his will, he left all his plates and pots and sil-
verware to Robert," said Adrienne. "Did you know
that?"

No, I hadn't known.

At the end of the evening, Adrienne took out her camera. She wanted a picture of all of us together, a memento of an evening that had been important to the
three of us.

On my way home, driving through Brooklyn's quiet
streets, I thought again of Vincent taking Robert's photograph over his objections and then keeping it all these
years. As time went on, Vincent needed that picture. As
the world receded, it comforted Vincent to keep his
sights set on those who had mattered to him. If he could
keep his important people with him, he would not die so
alone.

Later he had a dream that haunts me more than all the
others. "Dreamt that Robert came to visit me. I lived on
an island where the mail was parachuted down & sometimes it missed. Ronny was there."

Passionate grief does not link us with the
dead but cuts us off from them. . . . when I
feel the least sorry . . . H. rushes on my mind
in her full reality, her otherness. Not . . . all
foreshortened and patheticized and solem-
nized by my miseries, but as she is in her
own right.

C. S. LEWIS
A Grief Observed

—∞—

People do not die immediately for us, but
   remain bathed in a sort
of aura of life. . . . It is as though they were
   traveling abroad.

MARCEL PROUST

By early 1994, death was never far from Vincent's thoughts. He put himself to sleep by counting dead friends, and woke up thinking about them. "Probably be seeing Ronny soon," he wrote one morning. "If I live to see the end of the year I'll be lucky." Knowing Vincent as I had for ten diary-years, I expected that as he got closer to his own death, he would bunker himself, retreating from the living and the dying alike.

But he didn't. Vincent had always been very connected to his sisters. He had lived three thousand miles away for twenty years, but they were daily presences in his thoughts and made appearances in his dreams three or four nights a week. Wherever he went, he came back with gifts for them. While he never explicitly speculated about how his death would affect them, he did feel guilty he hadn't been honest with all of them all along.

For the first time, during this year, he even began to think about his relationship to his parents—"Mother" and "Father"—from whom he'd kept so much distance for so long.

"Being high made me think about things which made me worry," he wrote one night, sprawling on his couch, after smoking a joint. "Also kept thinking about me not being around much longer. Then started worrying about being w/family. I really have alienated myself."

On one of his last trips to Europe, he had read Amy Tan's novel *The Kitchen God's Wife*. Though his diary was filled with references to museums he visited and plays he saw, he managed to finish the book in three days, and it was on his mind for weeks thereafter. When he alluded to it, he sometimes referred to its author as "Amy," so clearly had she moved him. "Excellent," he wrote when he began it. The character "has MS but has not told her mother. I can relate. Glad I got the book." He certainly could relate. Not only did his parents not know he was HIV positive, they didn't even know (or at least he'd never told them) he was gay. He'd been living on disability for two years, and they didn't know that either. All they knew was that he was out of a job, and so they nagged him to look for one.

COULD HE GET CLOSER to his parents? Did he even want to? Whenever a concern was consciously on Vincent's mind, it often was dispatched to dreamquarters for further action. Soon after Vincent voiced his worry, his parents, especially his father, began to appear more frequently in his dreams. The dramatic theme, loosely speaking, was his family's need to safeguard a treasure, with Vincent always near or around the treasure. In finding his parents, or his connection to them, had he found a long-lost well-loved part of himself as well? Was the family treasure Vincent himself? He certainly wished he were.

Vincent's sisters didn't speak much of their brother's relationship with their father except to make it clear that Vincent had been the sensitive son of an insensitive man. "Vincent and my father weren't close," said Angela. Once, in nothing more than a burst of high spirits, Vincent, age eight, had put on Angela's stiff and crinkly crinoline and twirled about the room, making the girls giggle. His father, walking in on the hijinks, went after Vincent, his heavy hand raised.

Vincent, though, had never written his father off. At least in his dreams, now more than ever, he yearned to have his father know him and value him. "Dreamt that I was assisting my father to guard a famous painting by Goya." Two days later, "Dreamt that I was responsible for taking care of a diamond, my family its owner." And shortly thereafter, "Dreamt that my family owned a big house in the country & were renting part of it to a couple w/a little girl." But Vincent did not, or could not, open up to his parents—in fact, he rarely spoke to his father during his infrequent calls to his mother—and after a few weeks, his parents' brief stint as regulars in his dreamscapes ended.

Meanwhile, Vincent thought about his friendships, too. His oldest friends were all alive, but all, except for Robert, HIV positive. Joey, always the merriest, was now the happiest, too, but too far away to be any help. During the summer of 1991, walking down an Amsterdam street, Joey had struck up a conversation with a man named Jan. Love blossomed, and when Jan came to visit Joey in San Francisco a few months later, their relationship deepened. When Jan returned to his native Holland, Joey went with him. They seemed truly settled to Vincent, who spoke to Joey now and then on the phone. On one of Vincent's European trips, he visited them in Amsterdam. The walls were thin, and Vincent envied what he heard.

As for DDD, nothing much had changed with him. At best, Vincent could sometimes work his way from sour dislike up to tart ambivalence. DDD was still driving a flashy car, making lots of money, and hosting extravaganzas at his home every Fourth of July and Thanksgiving. He even showed off about his T cells. The higher the count, the healthier you were. A count below two hundred meant you had crossed the line from HIV positive into frank AIDS. "DDD called to brag that his T-cells are 850," wrote Vincent. "Mine only 300. Such a shmuck."

Then there was Eddy Cavello, who, like Joey, had been a guest at Vincent's long-ago Christmas dinner party and had cut his hair all these years. Eddy Cavello had tested positive a year after Vincent but his illness was devouring him in fast, hard bites. When he had the energy, he and Vincent volunteered at Open Hand delivering meals to homebound men with AIDS who were in worse shape than either one of them.

Recalling Vincent's numb race away from grief when Ronny died, I was expecting he would react the same way with Eddy. But again, I was wrong. Something new was happening to Vincent. Or something that had been happening in the wings was now onstage. A few months after his own diagnosis, Vincent became a member of a neighborhood group of HIV-positive men. He, Frank, Ruffin, Raphael, and Jeff met every few weeks to talk about their lives. Vincent never said a word of what they talked about or what he thought of the group. He only noted when he went, when he didn't, whose apartment it was at, and when the meeting was canceled.

But Vincent did announce the deaths of these men. With each death, those who were left showed up for the memorial service, in ever dwindling numbers. Vincent was most upset when Ruffin died. "Called Frank. . . . Discussed Ruffin's death. Frank told me that Ruffin's family . . . are not including us in his memorial. We'll do our own service. Don't get depressed."

But then Ruffin's family reconsidered. Vincent cooked two different kinds of rice casseroles, and during the memorial counted the house, pleased that twenty-seven people had shown up. "Some women, some straight, a few strange, all grieving over the death of Ruffin. Allowed to take some of his photos. I took four."

Then Eddy Cavello became ill. Over the years of cutting Vincent's hair (and selling him pot) they had become friends. I couldn't tell much about him from Vincent's account, except that their friendship was without either the tensions or intensity he'd had in his relationship with Joey. But with Joey now living in Amsterdam, Eddy had become more important.

By the start of '94, Eddy Cavello was much sicker than Vincent. Eddy's face, hands, arms, and legs were covered with swarms of red KS lesions, which he made no effort to cover up. Vincent was flooded with compassion for Eddy but could not bring himself to tell Eddy about his own lesions, all on parts of his body he could keep covered.

Vincent was away for a month during Christmas of 1993, visiting his family in New York. Two days after he got back, on Saturday, the eighth of January, Vincent found out that Eddy was at Laguna Honda, a hospital with a hospice program. I didn't know whether Eddy was in a hospital unit or the hospice unit because Vincent didn't say. "Oh dear," Vincent wrote. "Not surprised. Must visit him." And the next day, he did, although he had to take a bus and train there and back. "He looks awful," Vincent wrote that night, back home after his first visit. "A little [in]coherent. Peed in his bed. Could not deal with it."

This was what I expected, but his next line wasn't. "Must go back and visit." And he did. He went on Wednesday, and he went Friday, and he went again on Sunday, forty-five minutes each way, each visit difficult because in Eddy Cavello, Vincent saw himself.

As ever, he was the gift giver, just as he had been with Ronny, just as he had always been, probably even on that long ago winter day in my classroom. Whenever he visited Eddy, he arrived at his hospital room with a little something—a newspaper or pizza, a magazine or ice cream. He brought Eddy a fuchsia plant. He bought him a radio. "Glad I spent $15 for a better model," he noted.

Sometimes his impulse to give extended beyond material items. For a while, Eddy's hospital roommate was a man from Portland, Oregon, whose sister came to visit for a few days. On her last day, she stayed so long Vincent was afraid she would miss her flight back home. Knowing his way around the city, he got her to the airport shuttle just in the nick of time. Maybe he was thinking of Angela, Adrienne, and Sandra?

On a visit one Friday, he told Eddy he would be back at the end of the following week. But he couldn't stay away. Two days later he was back again. "Eddy to be home by Wednesday," he wrote that day. "Good."

Meanwhile Vincent was grappling with worsening news about himself. The day before he gave Eddy the radio, Vincent had called Dr. Raszyl to find out the results of lab tests he took periodically. "He called back by noon. My T-cells have dropped from 49–37. Great! And I have some parasite in my blood. Fuckin' great. It can cause damage to my brain. Now I need drugs that may lower my T-cells even further. Help! Called Frank who explained that I shouldn't freak out. Too late. Called Dr. Jacobs for KS procedure next Monday."

The very next line came without segue—"Called A.G. to convert 8 mil film into video"—but I knew how Vincent was thinking. If he was going to die, he wanted another realm to live in, he wanted to be forever piping and forever young. This was the film that he had made several years earlier in his filmmaking class, written by Vincent, starring Vincent, directed by Vincent. Converting it from film to the more accessible video was like putting down at his door a welcome mat for the world. Except for one thing: he couldn't find the film. "Started looking for my movie in closet," he wrote on February 18. "Tear the place apart. Still cannot find."

Meanwhile, for reasons Vincent didn't explain, Eddy Cavello didn't go home on Wednesday as planned. Nor did he go home in February, or March or April. Eddy was weakening, and as he did, Vincent's devotion deepened.

AS THE WEATHER WARMED, Vincent began to think about how to get Eddy out of the hospital for the day. He didn't know how to drive, so he enlisted Rhonda, an old friend from work, and on a beautiful clear Sunday morning in March the two of them arrived at Laguna Honda in Rhonda's red convertible. Getting Eddy out even for the day was like getting a ship through canal locks, but eventually they maneuvered him and his wheelchair through the bureaucracy and out the hospital doors. Then, radio blasting and the wind in their hair, they were on their way, heading over the Golden Gate Bridge to Marin County.

Truly, it was a joyride. With Eddy navigating, they found their way to a restaurant in Tiburon called Sam's where they waited almost two hours to get a seat for lunch. But they didn't seem to mind. By five, Eddy was back at Laguna Honda, and Vincent was back at home. The outing invigorated him, and for the first time in a long time, he was hungry when dinnertime came.

For the rest of March and April, Vincent was steadily attentive to Eddy, though his friend's continuing deterioration depressed him. During the first two weeks of May, though, Vincent was busier and more upbeat than usual, and with good reason. Tuesday, May 10 was Vincent's fortieth birthday, and the surrounding days were marked by celebrations, all intensified by his joy at having made it to forty at all. Half a dozen of his former coworkers from Eckert & Hauser took him to lunch, and another day, so did Carol. Robert from Atlanta sent a card, Joey sent chocolates and a T-shirt from Amsterdam, and Angela, Adrienne, and Sandra sent gifts, too. Vincent continued to search his apartment for the missing movie, and his best present to himself was that finally he found it. In his closet, just as he'd thought. "Found my movie in an envelope sandwiched between the magazines," he wrote. "So happy. Convert to video ASAP @ any cost."

As another birthday present, he treated himself to three days in Yosemite, leaving on the ninth. "HAPPY BIRTHDAY!" he wrote to himself in big bold letters on awakening the next morning. He relished his time away, reading, resting, strolling about, his diary in hand. He picked up a bird feather and dandelion and tucked them between the pages where I would find them.

VINCENT WAS BACK IN San Francisco on May 11, and once again Eddy Cavello was on his mind. On the afternoon of the thirteenth, he arrived at Laguna Honda for his first visit since the second. "Not in his room. New name. Visited nurse's station. He passed away, May 5, 1994. He never made it to his 40th B.D. I cried. He's one of my oldest and closest friends. Later found out from his father funeral services were this morning. No one told me. He was upset. Must send card w/photos. Needed to talk to someone. Called Rose. Felt better. Still upset."

Saturday, he went to Grace Cathedral and lit a candle for Eddy.

Sunday, he treated himself to lunch out at a new restaurant, noting "Eddy had wanted to eat there." Over the years, he had taken photos of Eddy. Eddy smiling. Eddy looking healthy. Eddy cutting hair. He'd never put them in albums, but he'd piled them all in boxes labeled by year. After his own private memorial luncheon for Eddy, Vincent went through his photo boxes putting aside several to send to Eddy's father. "So many people in my photos have passed on," he wrote. "Soon all I will be will be a photo."

Monday, he needed to talk some more about Eddy, so he called his friend Hilde.

Tuesday, he mailed Eddy's father a sympathy card.

The following Sunday, May 22, Vincent had a dream that included Eddy. "1st dream about Eddy. He was wearing a suit, was dealing w/S.S. A lady from the ROTC wanted him to join. Saw Ted Marris," an acquaintance who'd died, "trudging up my hill. Told Hilde that I saw him. Lights not working in my apt. Mother fixed them."

The next day, Monday, the twenty-third, Vincent decided to make a panel in memory of Eddy for the AIDS quilt, as he had for Ronny, only this time he systematically enlisted his friends from work to help him. "Sharon called. Told her about Eddy. She'll do a letter for his panel. Later in the day, Vincent heard from Rhonda, who'd helped him take Eddy on his last outing. "She'll help me w/a letter." In the next few days, Vincent found three others who signed on for letters as well. On Thursday the twenty-sixth, Vincent had a dream: he was singing "You'll Never Walk Alone."

On June 1 Vincent began his entry above the line, in the space in his diary where national holidays were noted. "TODAY IS EDDY'S 40TH B.D," he wrote.

—∞∞∞—

BY NOW, MY FAMILY was even sicker of Vincent than they had been at Cape Cod. For a while Reamy referred to him as The Man Who Came to Dinner but now he had taken to muttering about The Man Who Came to Dinner, Breakfast, Lunch, Dinner, and Breakfast.

In fact, everyone in my family thought Vincent was taking too much of my time. I did, too, except that I continued to be completely engaged with him in the intense way that I sometimes am with people—real or fictional—I've met only in books. It was a little bit like being in love. Or having a new baby.

One time Reamy, Paul, and Gabe sat in the car in the driveway, fuming, taking turns honking and waiting for me because I was busy with some last minute bit of Vincentiana. When I came out, whatever it was was stuffed in my bag. One way or another, Vincent was always with us.

Inside the house it was worse.

My study already looked as if it were as much Vincent's as mine, but now, stealthily and steadily, his possessions were making themselves at home in the rest of the house.

His diaries. His letters, ticket stubs, and bus tickets. His photos and feathers and flowers. I knew this man now, but his notes from his friends beginning "Dear Jimmy" reminded me there were still vast realms of his life I didn't know about and would never know about.

One night, Vincent kept my husband and sons out of the kitchen, his diaries and papers on piles on the table. I told them we would be having our dinner in the dining room instead. After some semi-serious harrumphing, they conceded this change in our routine and settled for dinner in the dining room. But when I brought up my insight *de jour* about Vincent, their interest was at best chilly.

"Uh-huh," said Reamy in the way he does when he's not really listening. He kept his eyes on his plate.

Paul rolled his eyes and kept eating.

"When are you going to be *done* with him?" asked Gabe, methodically pulverizing his peas with his fork.

I knew I wasn't done with him yet. Vincent's diary pages still pulsated for me, and there was less than a volume between me and the day when they would go flat and blank like an EKG monitor when the heartbeat stops. In bringing Vincent to life for myself, I had gotten to where I wanted to but I didn't know how. What if I couldn't carry the tune when his music ended?

I was impressed with him now. Just as his life was closing down, he was opening up, letting life in, becoming porous in a way he had resisted for so long, maybe for his entire life. When Ronny died, Vincent had gone drunk and numb. That I understood. But this time around, he was different. He had admitted loss. He had achieved misery.

I thought he was doing something else as well. Eddy at his late stages was not the Eddy that Vincent had known and been friends with. Late-Stage Eddy was someone who peed in his bed, whose eyes rolled back in his head, who curled up like a fetus, who, eventually, couldn't carry on a sensible conversation. This was not the Eddy that Vincent would want to remember, not the Eddy that anyone else who loved him would want to remember, and certainly not the Eddy that Eddy himself would want remembered. To let Eddy live, Vincent had to let Eddy die. To get the real Eddy back, Vincent had to let Late-Stage Eddy go. However one did that.

I had to learn what Vincent had apparently learned, maybe even learn it *from* him, if I was ever going to be able to properly remember my grandmother, or to have a broader emotional palette for the portrait of my father I carried around with me in my head, or to keep a genuine sense of my lifelong relationship to my mother even after she died. Now that I thought of it, and I was wishing that I hadn't, Late-Stage Eddy reminded me a little of my mother now.

If there was anything that was central to my mother's

identity, it was her car, an emblem of her fierce inde-
pendence. Like a '50s hot-rodder, she referred to her car
as her "wheels," and from the time I was seven, she'd
never been without one, naming them like pets—Puffing
Billy or Clementine—and endowing them with fairly
complex personalities. But now she had decided it was
time to hang up her keys.

"I'm not going to be driving anymore," she told me
this time when I came. "I was at a red light on Utica
Avenue the other day, and when the light turned green I
went blank. I had no idea why I was in my car or where
I was going."

With car, memories, and more going or gone, my
mother was relentlessly focused on whether she was still
herself. "Am I still me?" she asked. "Or am I just old
now?"

Another day, she came at it another way. "You don't
love who I am now, you love who I've been." Begging
the question of whom I did or did not love, it was certainly true that most of the time now she was not who
she'd been. I had known her my whole life, and of
course she had changed over that time, but in all that
time, she had always been herself, or at least some version of herself.

But often now she wasn't. Many of the most pro-
nounced aspects of her personality were gone—her com-

petence and eye for detail. Her generosity and humor. She, who prided herself on being a stellar bookkeeper, forgot to pay her bills or her numbers were wrong. Her generosity was eroded. "I'm not giving Christmas presents this year," she announced with a sour brusqueness. More and more, she seemed not to sit squarely in herself. She rarely referred to herself as "I" anymore. Instead, she referred to herself in the third person, as "The Old Bag." When she had first begun to depart from herself, I had decided quite explicitly that what I had to do was continue to recognize her, persist in addressing her as if she were whom she had always been. I thought her sense of dignity and her sense of selfhood required that kind of confirmation.

It was a struggle, but sometimes it worked.

One day, when I came to visit, I was feeling particularly preoccupied by departmental stresses at work, which made the atmosphere tense for everyone.

"What's wrong?" she said, as I took off my coat. "I can see it on your face."

"I'm really hating going to work, " I told her, making an effort to explain.

"Oh, dear," she said, after listening attentively to the details. "That must be very hard to put up with. Isn't there anything you can do about it?"

"No, not really," I said glumly.

When it was time to leave, I stood up to put my coat on and button it.

She, too, got up from the couch where she'd been sitting, walked over to me, and straightened the collar of my coat in a way she hadn't since I was eight.

"It will be all right," she said soothingly, as if I had scraped my knee. I didn't cry until I was in the car.

The number of people capable of recognizing her as who she had been was now whittled down to my sister and me and our families. We had struck a deal where she could continue to live in her house but only if she had ever-increasing support—"my keepers" she called them —provided by people who had never known her when she wasn't, relatively speaking, Late-Stage Eddy. Joan was still my mother's mainstay, with two or three other women as well. They cared for her gently and with great sensitivity to her feelings, but every once in a while, when she balked at eating, they couldn't help falling into that cajoling little singsong tone one uses with truculent toddlers —"c'mon, let's have just one more bite of this yummy sandwich"—which only made my mother more truculent. "You've got to get food into her," said her physician, as if he were talking about a picnic cooler.

Eddy Cavello had also gone from being himself to becoming a ruin of himself. How had Vincent navigated his dying and death? I went back and studied sections of his diaries as if they were Cliff's Notes and the final exam was coming soon.

While Vincent had fled from Ronny, he'd ministered to Eddy.

While he'd gone numb with Ronny, he'd let himself feel sad for Eddy. (And yes, a lot of his sadness for Eddy was sadness for himself, but did that really matter?)

Afterwards, he turned to photographs of the real Eddy.

He even reenacted the real Eddy, *became* him, by eating at a restaurant Eddy would have eaten at.

He didn't keep Eddy's death a secret; he talked about it as often as he needed to, if necessary, buttonholing people to listen.

In deciding to do a panel in memory of Eddy, he'd found a way to recognize Eddy's life. He'd done this for Ronny, too, but with Eddy, Vincent had actually built himself an ad hoc community of Sharon, Rhonda, Hilde, and a few others. They would support him through this period and they would recognize him as someone bereaved.

THIS WAS A TRIUMPH for Vincent—and for Eddy. If there was a danger that Eddy would be remembered as a ruin, there was also a danger he would survive as a saccharine version of someone he'd never been. I'd seen that happen once when I was a child, and I'd never forgotten it. At the time, I couldn't voice what bothered me, but every time I looked at the picture of my friend Karen's Aunt Roberta on her hallway wall, I got a funny twisted feeling of discomfort in my stomach.

Aunt Roberta—even I called her that—was a high-spirited, brusque cigarette smoker with salt-and-pepper hair and a raspy rat-a-tat laugh. She had no kids, but she was a figure and a force in the lives of her nieces and nephews. She went to the racetrack, she wore bright red lipstick, and she played pinochle for money every Friday night with her brother, who was Karen's father, and a few other men. So did her husband, Uncle Pete. I liked Aunt Roberta a lot. She told dirty jokes and let us listen and laughed louder than we did, slapping her knee as she laughed, her unfiltered Camel dangling from the corner of her mouth.

Then Aunt Roberta got lung cancer and did most of her dying at Karen's house, in a recliner in front of a television set in their dining room, a dark room with heavy mahogany furniture. She didn't laugh anymore, she smelled funny, and something dark happened around her eyes. Then she died. Soon after her death a photograph of her appeared on a wall on my friend's staircase, its frame pale pink, pale green, and heart shaped. In the frame was a smaller photograph of Aunt Roberta also cut out in the shape of a heart, and it was pasted on a condolence card cut to fit the frame that said in ornate lavender script, "Gone but not Forgotten."

The photograph of Aunt Roberta was taken one summer day at the beach. She was wearing a bathing suit and standing in the ocean pretty far from shore, though the water was no higher than her ribs. From where she stood, she was waving to the onshore photographer. It was like she was waving from heaven or something. To me the display didn't evoke Aunt Roberta, it hid her. Of all the ways you could bring Aunt Roberta back to life, or evoke the life she had lived and who she had been, this was the wrongest one possible. This wasn't Aunt Roberta, it was room deodorizer. The right photograph would have shown her in the kitchen, playing cards with the guys, a Bud label stuck in a corner of the frame.

ONCE, MANY YEARS EARLIER, I had seen a father and his two young sons encircled by their small church community as they mourned a wife and mother they'd loved and took the first small steps to putting her back together in a way that seemed right. Claudia, the wife of Reamy's close friend Hank, had died of breast cancer at forty—Vincent's age when he died—leaving Hank and their twin six-year-old boys, Ian and Nicholas. For us, as Claudia's friends, her terribly premature death saddened us. For us as parents, though, it was terrifying to sit in that church, all of us sodden with sympathy for these two small vulnerable brothers who sat there wide-eyed and blank in a way I recognized all too well.

We lived in New York and Claudia and Hank lived in Boston, but we had followed Claudia's condition closely. She had first been diagnosed right after Labor Day; then declined with dizzying speed throughout the year. Every piece of news was bad.

Claudia died right after the next Labor Day, a year following her diagnosis.

Throughout that year, she was open and direct about her illness, and she'd let you in as much as you could stand it with details about her chemotherapy, radiation, nausea, and hair loss. On Claudia's last visit to us early in the summer, she and Hank had dinner with us in our apartment. With summer and cooking, the room was hot, and we had no air conditioning.

"Hoooh," Claudia said, plucking off her wig with one hand and wiping the sweat off her bald head with the other. Then she placed the wig on the table as if it were a tea cozy, and there it sat through dessert. I was shocked at first, but relieved by her directness. For me it was more welcome than silence or secrecy would have been.

Two months later, Claudia died at home, as she had wanted. The day after she died, Reamy and I went to

Boston for her funeral. When I went to the bathroom at their home and closed the door, I saw her white nightgown with embroidered pink flowers still hanging on a hook on the back of the door, wrinkled and badly stained. In the chaos of events, no one would have thought to remove it. Claudia's wig on my table had made me face her illness, but her nightgown had sucked me into her dying. At that moment, whatever feelings I had had —sorrow, regret, pain for Claudia's children, sympathy for Hank—fled from the stained nightgown and went into hiding. Removing the nightgown might have spared Hank and the boys just a bit, but I was so frozen I didn't even think of it.

The next day was the funeral, and Hank had made arrangements for Claudia's ashes to be entombed in the church wall right behind the altar as she had requested. In the procession down the church aisle to the entombment wall—family leading, friends following—fairness prevailed. Each son carried a ceramic jar he had made in pottery class, and in each receptacle reposed precisely half of Claudia's ashes, scrupulously divided into two piles by Hank that morning as Ian and Nicholas looked on. Claudia, always careful to treat each twin fairly, would have understood and she would have approved.

The next evening, Claudia's friends returned to the church. By night, it had the comfortable feel of a coffeehouse

—recessed lighting, a raised platform now cleared of the altar, and behind it the sandblasted brick wall where Claudia's ashes were now entombed. Seats surrounded what was now a stage on three sides, so we all could see one another.

There these friends of Claudia's sat around informally and talked about her, her love for Ian and Nicholas, her love for Hank, her eye for design, her community spirit.

Then one woman told a story about the last time she and Claudia had driven to the mall to do some shopping. They had piled into the van with their packages and were just heading back to pick up the kids from school when Claudia remembered a phone call she just had to make. Just had to.

"Well all right," said the friend, pulling up to a pay phone in the parking lot, "but let's try to keep it short."

There was a murmur of hesitant laughter. Claudia had been admirable in many ways, but at times she was garrulous beyond endurance. God forbid she got you on the phone; it was impossible to get off. So the friend sat in her car, drumming her fingers on the steering wheel and waiting while Claudia made her call. Then she waited some more.

"Finally," she said, "Claudia came back. 'So?' I said. 'Obviously, you got whatever it was all worked out?'"

"Oh no," Claudia had said, now fully engrossed in

snapping her seat belt. "She wasn't even in. I just left a brief message."

Other stories followed, her friends' efforts to do battle with the devastating illness that had not only killed Claudia but threatened to obscure her to them. Story by story, the laughter grew more robust, warming us. It also summoned back Claudia as I had known her, paradoxically allowing me then to acknowledge her death, to feel sad, in a way I hadn't since the sight of her stained nightgown had frozen me. I put into words now what I had come to understand watching Vincent with Eddy: to let the dead live, you must let the dead die. For Claudia's family, there was mourning ahead to be sure. But in that moment, the miracle of resurrection had also begun.

Unknowing I understand:
I too am written,
and at this very moment
someone spells me out.

OCTAVIO PAZ
"Brotherhood"

———oøøo———

IT WAS NOW THE summer of 1994. Time was running out, and Vincent knew it. He had a frank case of AIDS, and he was weak and in pain most of the time. Nevertheless, he was determined to live fully what life was left to him—"live while you can," he wrote in his diary—and in October, as I watched in admiration, he gamely set off for a three-week trip to Europe. In his earlier trips his diary was thick with mementos and photos as if he wanted to have the experience after the trip rather than during it. But this time, he seemed to be trying to engage with each moment, each experience. He toured actively but saved little.

Despite his pluck and his gumption, it was a taxing

trip. After staying a week in Paris with Jean Marc, an old friend who worked for Air France, Vincent traveled to Dresden, Stuttgart, Innsbruck, Prague, and Budapest. He was constipated and in pain, and although he layered his feet in Band-Aids, they bled all the time, staining his socks. As a final piece of misery, he broke a tooth. Back in Paris, he went to mass at Notre Dame and was so tired he fell asleep in the pew.

Once Vincent was back from Europe, his deterioration hastened. Angela saw him in November on his way back from Europe and thought he looked sort of all right, but when she saw him in Brooklyn at Christmas, she was horrified at how thin and sallow he had become in just six weeks. With Vincent in December 1994 and me in December 1995, he had almost caught up to me, although of course he never would.

My Christmas that year was a hard one. Everywhere I looked there was loss. There was no card from Vincent, of course, and no card from my mother either because she didn't remember it was Christmas. I'd always given her books and pretty calendars as Christmas presents, but one evening when I called her, she told me the books would have to stop.

"I'm not reading any more. When I open a book to where I left off, I can't remember what I've already read."

Then she told me she had decided not to come to my sister's for Christmas Day, a tradition in our family for twenty years that began with the birth of my first niece, the first of my mother's four grandchildren. "I'm too old, and I'm too tired," said my mother. "I don't want the children to see me like this, and I don't have the energy to perform for a whole day."

"C'mon. We'll pick you up."

"You always pick me up."

"We'll take you home earlier."

"If I don't go, then you won't have to interrupt your day."

I cajoled, and when that failed, I badgered, and when that didn't work either, I got angry. Nothing worked.

"The old order changeth, yielding place to new."

She actually said that. She didn't even say "yielding way," which is what people who say things like that would say. But she was right. I checked *Bartlett's Quotations*. She'd always found it easy to memorize, dating back to when she'd learned "The Charge of the Light Brigade" in sixth grade. Over the years, I'd heard her recite dozens of poems and scores of dramatic monologues. Often her own memories took the form of recalled conversations. Even now, despite the fact that she seemed to be living without a rearview mirror to anything that had happened more than two minutes earlier, the part of her brain where she stored all that talk remained completely intact. I imagined some closet in her brain, safe and dry, where she stored those lines, ribbons tightly wound on spools that at a moment's notice she could find and unfurl like so many brightly colored kite tails in the breeze.

Tonight it had been those lines from Tennyson. Later that evening in my study, just for the hell of it, I blew the dust off an old volume of Tennyson (two shelves up from Vincent's shelf), which I hadn't opened since graduate school. The longest poem in it was "In Memoriam," which Tennyson was first impelled to write as a way of coming to terms with the death of his best friend, Arthur H. Hallam.

I remembered the poem largely because it was interminable, but also because when I first read it, I was twenty-four, the same age Tennyson was at Hallam's death. At that age, the idea that a friend could die was unthinkable to me. The two had become close at Cambridge four years earlier, so much so that Hallam got to know Tennyson's sister, fell in love with her, and became engaged. But while Hallam was in Paris with his father, he had some sort of seizure, and he died a few hours later. Tennyson was so shocked and devastated that even weeks later, once his friend's body had been returned to England, he couldn't bring himself to go to the funeral.

In the finished poem (which it took Tennyson twenty years to complete to his satisfaction), he took the reader through two years in his life—starting with his acute grief at Hallam's death and the first Christmas without him, looking where he was by the second Christmas, and culminating with his recovery and acceptance by the third Christmas.

As I stood browsing at my bookshelf, Reamy wandered into the room to see what I was up to, so I compared my memory of the poem with his.

"Did you know that Queen Victoria kept a copy of 'In Memoriam' at her bedside after her husband Prince Albert died?" he asked.

I knew that for years after her beloved Albert's death, she laid out fresh clothes for him every single morning because it made her feel better to do so, and I also knew that after "In Memoriam" was published, the queen and Tennyson became friends, but I didn't know anything about what she read alone in her bed at night.

"It consoled her."

I continued to stand at my bookshelf leafing through the poem, coming across a stanza toward the end that leapt out at me. In it, now beyond mourning, Tennyson describes how he feels as he rereads letters from Hallam, dead at this point for several years:

> So word by word, and line by line,
> > The dead man touch'd me from the past,
> > And all at once it seem'd at last
> His living soul was flash'd on mine.

My sentiments exactly! This stanza was there the last time I read it? Once again I saw the same impossible blurring of the boundary between death and life, the same instantaneous transit between past and present that I'd first felt reading Vincent's letter to me. Two words rubbed together to create the spark of life.

Whatever else the poem was, it was a description of the ongoing relationship of the living to the dead that continues after swollen grief subsides. Such relationships weren't just my concern, and they weren't just Vincent's, either.

———

ONE MILD AUGUST AFTERNOON, Vincent was out shopping for groceries. He'd made it a daily activity now because this way he had less to lug back. Standing at the foot of Clay contemplating the two increasingly steep hills he'd have to hike up to get back to his apartment, he saw an old acquaintance. "Ran into Jim on Polk," he wrote as soon as he got back. "He said that he was just thinking of me. I know that he knows about me & that I know about him. Wonder how much longer he's got & he's thinking the same about me."

That same week he mentioned that Joey's old friend Jared had died.

The week after, he mentioned that an acquaintance, Denny Ford, would be having a garage sale, and Vincent mused about when he might have his own.

These garage sales Vincent alluded to now and then initially puzzled me until I realized that he seemed to take them as coded announcements: someone was on disability and selling his stuff off to get a little extra money, or someone was admitting his days were numbered and was unloading his earthly possessions.

The garage sale, if indeed others understood it as he did, was but one among a swarm of accommodations gay San Franciscans had in place to manage death. There were others: hospices, grief groups, and food delivery. Then there were obituaries, private memorials, and public memorials—the individual life celebrated, the collective life of the community defiantly affirmed.

Living in a community so consumed by death, dying, and memory, Vincent did not go numb or burn out or tune out, as one might have expected and as many probably did. Instead, with some of the chaotic element of death perhaps removed via collective planning, he learned what it took to mourn and to get to the terrain beyond mourning. And he knew it better with Eddy than he'd known it with Ronny.

Vincent identified with Eddy in a way he hadn't with Ronny—because his grief for Eddy was also his grief for himself. But keeping Eddy alive was a triumph, too, because it allowed him to feel hopeful about what he could expect from the living (for instance, me) once it was his turn to be dead.

Opening his heart to a dying man he identified with was but a first step. If he wanted to outwit oblivion, he was going to have to take the next step and open up to the living. That was going to be hard, perhaps the hardest thing he'd ever done. It required a bravery he'd never had, which was why so much of his life was so lonely in the first place.

If Vincent couldn't open up to the living, he was truly doomed. But he also knew better than those who would survive him what they would have to do to help keep him alive in their hearts once he was dead. Now the living man he was had to make the decisions for the dead man he would become.

Vincent's position as a living man who would be dead

and a dead man who now reached out to the living made me realize that other people as well were stumbling around looking for ways to manage their relationships with the dead in their lives. But this territory beyond grief was so uncharted it didn't even have a name.

One of those looking around was my friend Donna Bassin, whose younger sister died when she was a child of seven or eight, leaving Donna with a persistent interest in mourning and memorializing. As an adult, she had become a psychologist and psychoanalyst, adding another perspective to her interest. She had once told me that she thought Freud's understanding of mourning was much too limited. Maybe even wrong. Freud believed that when someone died, you simply drew your emotional connection to that person back into yourself, sort of like winding in a fishing reel once you'd lost the fish. That was when all went well, Freud thought. But if you'd had a good deal of anger toward the person who'd died, then you might be in for trouble. That anger could invade you. It could ferment and turn grief into depression.

In Donna's own view, mourners, at least those who had mastered the process of grieving, found ways to convert, not curtail, their relationships with the dead person. They could infuse their emotions for the person they loved into activities that summoned that fullness of feeling. This redirection of emotions was a living act of memorial. Maybe that's what Donna herself was doing. And maybe in writing about Vincent I was, in part, reckoning with my own losses.

While I was reading Vincent's diaries, I read an article in the *New Yorker* by Alexander Stille about the Kitawan, a tribe living on an island off New Guinea. When the grown son of an elderly tribesman died, his father boiled his skull in a pot and drank the soup made from the head. This was a bereft father's effort to keep his son with him, now and forever, not so different from what Christians taking Communion—*communion*—hoped for. After that, the family kept their son's skull in their home. From time to time, the father would take out the filial cranium from wherever he kept it and hold it contemplatively in both hands, as if it were a photo album.

My next-door neighbor Joanne had on her fireplace mantle a box with a big skull painted on the front against a black background. The box was about one cubic foot in dimension, and the skull front was actually two symmetrical doors opening outward. Inside was a diorama—in its center was a skeleton (with long, neon pink hair) sitting up rather happily in her coffin, while around her were four or five additional skeleton people who did not appear even remotely troubled by this event.

Joanne said she'd picked it up for ten dollars the last time she was in Mexico.

It was folk art connected to *el Dia de los Muertos,* the Day of the Dead, a festive Mexican holiday in early November during which the living cheerfully devote themselves to the dead people in their lives in a day of celebration and remembrance said to go back to the Aztecs and Mayans.

Whatever its date in the distant past, the holiday has long been celebrated on November 2, right near its more sober companion, All Saints' Day. While skeleton art is available every day, on November 2, bakers bake special pastry, some with the top shaped like skeleton faces (sometimes with the name of the dead written in icing), florists sell the marigolds associated with the day, and families go in droves to the graves of their dead.

No one shows up empty-handed. The relatives come bearing gifts: favorite meals, clothing, CDs, or even sporting equipment. They picnic, they plant flowers. Not mourning or haunted or numb, they've made a place on their cultural map celebrating the living presence of the dead in the lives of the living.

Donna had been in Mexico several times for the Day of the Dead. On her last visit, while she strolled through a cemetery, she stopped to chat with a plump middle-aged woman who was sitting on a folding chair in the middle of a cemetery plot (her mother's, as it turned out) watching the Mexican equivalent of *Dallas* on her tiny battery-run television.

"This was Mama's favorite program," the woman explained, gesturing in the direction of the TV, which she had nestled in the grotto of her mother's headstone.

"Do you think your mother is watching the program with you?" Donna asked.

"I don't think she can actually hear this broadcast," she said after a brief pause, "but watching it here makes me feel like she's with me."

Does staying connected to the dead mean *doing* something? For many, it seems so. Recently, my mother remarked that everyone she knew was either dead or in Florida. Her phrasing made me think about how some people do treat death as if it were a state somewhere *near* Florida. This was most striking to me in the "In Memoriam" section of the *New York Times,* where every day four or five people write the equivalent of wish-you-were-here postcards to the dead. Today, I found one that said, "Dear Mom, I will always love you and treasure your memory." It was signed, "Your Son, Robbie."

Outdoor shrines—at the site of fatal accidents, for instance—seem to have proliferated. Meanwhile, in cyberspace, there are literally thousands of individual memorial web pages as well as memorial web rings. Most poignant in the wake of the attack on the World Trade Center has been the massive public grieving and memorializing on the streets and online. For a long time now, there has also been the sustained political and social activism initiated by mothers whose children have died tragically — Megan's Law, Mothers Against Drunk Driving, and more. And clearly there is an audience for all those movies in which a living person has an ongoing relationship with a well-loved dead person, *Ghost Dad* with Bill Cosby being just one example. Many of these movies are comedies, not horror films, and the source of the humor is that only the living person can see this friendly ghost.

Years ago, I had interviewed the poet Maggie Anderson about the stories in her family. Many of the relatives she'd told stories about had died when Maggie was very young, including her mother. "I'm very comfortable with the dead," she told me. "I have to be. So many people I know and love are on the other side. I'm not kidding, some of my best friends are dead."

My friend Joanne seems to feel the same way about her mother, who died suddenly one night twenty years ago shortly after leaving a party at Joanne's apartment. "She's still with me," Joanne told me. "I still have conversations with her every day."

And it isn't only her mother. "I always take a little piece of everyone with me, and it's always a physical gesture," she explained. "I hang up clothes on the line exactly the way my mother did and every time I do, I think of her." From others, living and dead, she has taken the way she sweeps a floor, ties a scarf, arranges flowers. All small gestures, but all gestures that furnish daily life. "I always feel everyone I love is with me," she said.

Vincent, too, had tried this—eventually—when he went to Eddy's favorite restaurant for lunch a few days after Eddy died. Though Vincent wasn't closest to me, of all my relationships with the dead, my connection to him was the surest. And this was true, even though I didn't know what he looked like or sounded like or smelled like or anything. It struck me then that our deepest sense of another person lives inside each of us, like some internal hologram, or maybe a physical feeling. All those people who so profoundly feel that the dead are somehow right there with them base their convictions on something more visceral than visual. When Joanne hung her clothes or Vincent sat in a restaurant sipping his tea or the Mexican lady watched her tiny TV in the graveyard, what they were doing was summoning their dead.

Of the dead in my midst, my grandmother was the person whose physical being I had always sensed most strongly. When I really tried, I could now find her—as a soothing gestalt of sensations and sense memories. She was the scent of Old Spice, the feel of pearly elderly skin, all this alloyed with the butternut crunch she gave me at Easter, and the coffee-flavored chewing gum she gave me when she sat at my bedside the whole day until the ambulance came because I was so sick I had to go to the hospital. My memories of her now were accompanied by sensations in my own body—a feeling of satiety right below my ribs, warmth that spread upward and culminated in the impulse to smile. The backdrop, because it was least powerful, was any of several visual images of her I had stored in my head. The physical sensations prompted by my thoughts of her must have been there during our earliest relationship decades ago.

Now that I thought about it, I had a similar and even stronger collection of memories about my mother—procedural memories, more like remembering how to ride a bike than remembering a bike ride I once took—and I had automatically drawn on them when I had become a mother myself. It was these ancient memories—housed more in my body than in my mind—that let me know, as if instinctively, how to soothe my boys as babies, how to talk in that loony crooning voice. In fact, mine was identical in both content and inflection to my mother's, which I quickly discovered when I saw my mother with my first son. It had been decades since I'd gone to my mother for physical comfort, but I could still effortlessly summon what my mother's hands felt like, cool on my head when I was sick as a child, and I knew it the way I knew my way home. The same, later on, with my husband's hands. And that must be why mothers and lovers, each so inextricably linked to visceral memory, live so powerfully and so enduringly within us.

Many years ago, I had interviewed Gilda Radner. I never thought of it till now, but once, during a long rehearsal break, she had told me how she kept her dead father with her. He had loved show business and that extended to the backyard performances done by Gilda, whom he adored. "I was just his favorite thing," she told me with that loopy smile of hers. He had become ill when she was twelve, and died when she was fourteen, leaving her bereft.

"Maybe I became a performer because I wanted to be what my father had loved so much." I put that in my article. That same afternoon, she also told me that she most strongly felt her connection to him when she performed, almost as if he were watching her. I left that part out of the article because at the time it sounded too weird to me. Now I know better.

My relationship with my own dead father was so lacking still. A year after he died—three years before I wrote about Gilda—I had a dream about him, about us, actually. At a store he no longer owned I went up a stairway that never existed. From the landing, I could see into a small windowless room bathed in yellowish light. On a folding canvas cot in the middle of the room sat my father.

On every wall were huge photographic images of me, blowups of actual waking-life pictures my father had once taken of me as a small child of three or four. These weren't prints hanging on the walls. They were painted onto the wall of this dim room. Definitely not portable. In one of them I was on a small wooden back porch peering through a screened door as I stood on my toes reaching for the handle. I knew it to be an old hunting lodge in upstate New York—on a tiny island in the Susquehanna River—which my father had bought years earlier and where we spent a few summers with an assortment of cousins and aunts. I remembered my time on Butternut Island as idyllic. In the photograph, I was dressed for a dewy summer morning in rubber boots, long pants, and a jacket, on my head a baseball cap, much too large and raffishly tilted. I'd seen the image hundreds of times in the photo album and it bespoke the photographer's tenderness toward his subject. My father's tenderness toward me.

And now in this dream a year after my father's death, this image and others in stark black and white were on the walls of his secret cell. I stood outside the door frame, deeply touched. I hadn't known about this secret room, this room of my father's, this room of mine, filled with images of me.

"Can I have these?" I asked.

"No," he said.

———— ◦◦◦ ————

IN VINCENT'S DIARY, IT was now a year before his death, and except for the fact that he obviously had left me his diaries, I still didn't see how he was going to be able to. My relationship with him was in pretty good shape (and why not?—he was meeting my needs, more so than I had ever expected) but when I thought back I saw in hindsight that even as early as the fall of 1992 his relationship with me had begun to deteriorate.

In the summer of '92, he'd been happy with me when awake and hopeful about me in his dreams. "Decided to visit Elizabeth Stone in the Village," he wrote one July morning on waking. "Found myself very early in the morning strolling through the streets. Passed a church where I took a Stone figurine. Went into a flower store, passed a coffee shop w/hot buns. Ended up by water. Dreamt that I woke up & relived the dream w/Gayle. Hated getting up."

It seemed to be a gratifying dream for Vincent, a twice-told tale with me cast as Our Lady of the Loaves and Flowers. Vincent stayed happy with me throughout the summer and even into the fall. When he went to Europe in September, he took me along in his thoughts. After decades of being content with our Christmas card toss, he even wanted to see me. In October he sent me a postcard from Frankfurt telling me he would be in New York for Christmas. "Maybe we can get together," he wrote.

I remembered that postcard from Frankfurt, and maybe that's when the trouble started. For one thing, in his diary, he was more tentative than I remembered him being his postcard. "We'll see," he wrote. On my first reading, I had missed what I now saw clearly. For Vincent "we'll see" used in the context of developing relationships really meant "forget it!" Had I done anything to upset him in 1992? I was pretty sure I hadn't, unless the fact that I hadn't tried to reach *him* during that Christmas period constituted a rejection. But I didn't think so. If I could have a relationship with him that he knew nothing about, so vastly separated by time and space, by life and death, then he could do the same with me. What I believe happened was that when he considered moving closer—showing me his diaries the way as a teenager in my backyard I had once shown mine to Richard—he got scared, as scared as he'd been at the prospect of getting closer to all those others before me.

Christmas cards were one thing. That was what friends

did. He could manage friendship, even close friendship. He'd done it for years with Joey. But his diaries? That was something else. That was intimacy. That was vulnerability. That was exposure. Even with all those unbridgeable separations between us, he was terrified. Sometimes you can hide but you can't run, and ultimately Vincent didn't. Was it because no one else could give him what he imagined I could give him? Maybe. I also thought his relationship with Eddy Cavello had been his best and most intimate so far, and it emboldened him, it let him stand still and tolerate his uncertainty—Should I stay or should I go?—rather than racing to the hills as he always had.

So he stood still, growing as his life shrunk, and dreamt uneasy dreams. "Dreamt that I was in NYC," he wrote a year later. "I was taking a class w/Elizabeth Stone but was too embarrassed to see her."

Six weeks later, he had another dream about me. "I was in NYC & about to meet Elizabeth Stone & her husband. She designed jewelry & he drove Rolls Royce. I was supposed to meet them in a bar, but woke up before Elizabeth turned around." Was this one a little more encouraging? I knew how Vincent dreamt. Jewels appeared in his dreams when he was yearning to feel valuable and important.

At the same time that Vincent was having trouble with

me, I couldn't help but notice he was making striking progress with others. As he headed into 1994, asleep and awake, he was opening up in ways I had not thought him capable of.

Most strikingly, he seemed to be inching toward self-acceptance or at least wishing for it. For six years, his KS lesions had obsessed him. By day, he had hidden in his clothing—sweatpants and a sweatshirt at the gym, and long-sleeved shirts outdoors, even in the heat. By night in his dreams, his lesions had been his scarlet letters.

But now he began to dream that he could reveal himself fully and still be accepted. "Dreamt I was at [work]," he wrote during the Christmas season of 1993. "Sharon was hemming my pants and did not flinch when she saw the KS lesion on my leg."

He also began to consider the possibility that he might be a decent man unjustly injured by AIDS rather than a pariah who had to lurk at the shadowy sidelines. "Dreamt that I was naked with Denny Ford," Vincent wrote in April of 1994, of a man he had been attracted to a few years earlier. "We were about to have sex but when he saw KS marks on my back, he said I looked like I was whipped."

He also dreamt he had fallen in love with a man he met after he'd lost his jacket and keys. "I kissed him. He kissed me back. He did not notice my lesions." The dream had his friend Carol as a protective and watchful presence: at its beginning, she appears, wanting to take him out for his birthday—his fortieth birthday—and at the end, she reappears, to find him.

The alteration in Vincent that allowed him to leave me his diaries was presaged, I believe, by a change in his relationship with Carol, who typed his deathbed letter to me and asked me to pray for him. They had worked together and been friends long before Vincent began his diaries, but during the diary years, their friendship was one of the occasional-lunch variety, at least according to Vincent's depiction. Carol kept Vincent informed about her life, but he kept her in the dark about his, especially his HIV status and the real reason he had stopped working at Eckert & Hauser. After Carol saw *Philadelphia* in early 1994, in which Tom Hanks plays an HIV-positive gay man in decline, she told him, "Oh Vincent, I thank God you're OK." He had not corrected her.

Vincent's main source of income was a modest monthly disability check, so when Carol offered him freelance work in her office, he took it eagerly. But in order to keep his secret (and perhaps cornered by questions he hadn't anticipated) he'd given Carol false information for the forms she'd had to fill out. Now he rightly feared that the discovery of his lies would get them both in trouble. He was biting a friendly hand, and he felt guilty.

"You must tell Carol everything," he admonished himself on March 10.

But when Carol called him up that day, his courage failed him.

"I should/must tell her in person," he rationalized.

A week and a half later, on Saturday the nineteenth, he still hadn't told her. "Keep thinking about Carol & how I lied to her. Will she freak out when I tell her the truth? . . . I gotta tell Carol everything. Tomorrow over the phone. Write everything down."

The next day, Sunday the twentieth, he was ready to go forward. "Waited until 10:00 A.M. to call Carol. [Her husband] answered. Carol not home. . . . Oh well." The middle of the day, he spent with Eddy Cavello. "He's losing it. . . . Will this be me? I want to go quickly and painlessly."

When he got home, Carol had not yet called back, so he gritted his teeth and called her again, and when the machine picked up, he gritted some more and left a message.

Late that night, Carol called back and finally they talked. "Gave her the speech," he wrote, distancing himself from what was most certainly a wrenching disclosure. "She cried. Then she told me that she will say that she forget to get my SS# so I did not need to tell her. Still glad I did."

And then, riding the momentum of his own bravery, Vincent popped the question: Would she willing to be the executrix for his will?

Carol said yes.

The next time Vincent saw Carol, he gave her a CD of the soundtrack to *Philadelphia,* an apt gift, which acknowledged not only his friendship, but his illness and his acceptance of his death. A few days after that, on the twenty-fifth, they met for lunch before going together to the lawyer's. "We chatted about everything," Vincent wrote. "Feel better I don't have to lie." In his diary for that day, I found a note from Carol he'd tucked in. "Dear Vincent," she wrote, "Thanks a lot for helping me out in this project. Also thanks a million for my 'Philadelphia' CD which will make me think of you (and how lucky I am to have a friend like you) each time I play Neil Young's song. Later alligator."

In opening up to Eddy, Vincent had opened up to the dying, but in opening up to Carol, he had at last opened up to the living, to those who would be here, when he no longer was, to do what he wanted done. It meant he was also prepared to be open with me—the first person who would see his diaries in their entirety and who might treat them as the jewels he hoped they were. I looked again at Vincent's letter to me still taped to the window in my study. He wanted me to write about him but he also wanted me to save his diaries from "the wrong hands." Whose hands could those be? What could any hands possibly do to him now that he was dead? It wasn't exposure he feared, but the opposite, I thought. He was counting on me to be the first reader but not the only reader.

As for what I might think of his life? In his last dream about me, I was still his teacher, but at least this time, he wasn't too embarrassed to see me. He was uncertain, yes, but confident enough to believe I wouldn't give him an F in life. "Dreamt that I walked into a classroom," he wrote. "Elizabeth Stone was there grading papers, but I could not see her face."

DURING THIS TIME, my mother broke her hip. Then she had a heart attack. Then she got pleurisy. Then she developed diabetes. For three months she was in the hospital spiraling downward with ever-increasing momentum. I was grieved, preoccupied, anxious. I ate too much and blew up too often. I needed a lot of help, and I got a lot of help from a lot of people.

But I also have to say that I was not a stranger in a strange land, and when I lost sight of my mother—and I did—I also found her again. I cried often, sometimes just because I could. As a result of my time traveling with

Vincent, I knew the terrain, and I knew what to do for my mother, and for myself, with surprising clarity. As I saw it, she wasn't living, she was being lived by a factory's worth of devices and medications. Most of the time she was too ill or too weak to talk. And sometimes she was just too confused—"Are you the one with the sons?" she asked me one day, to distinguish me from my sister, the one with the daughters. But some days, she found her way to oases of lucidity.

"Am I dying?" she asked one afternoon by way of openers.

I hedged. "Well, you've certainly had a rough time of it."

"But am I dying?"

"I don't know, Mom. Even the doctors don't know." That was true. Some thought she was, and some didn't.

She remained silent.

"You've had enough?" I asked.

"Even the weariest river winds somewhere safe to sea."

Swinburne. I looked it up later that day.

By this time, my mother had a doctor for just about every one of her bodily organs (possibly each kidney had its own doctor, I told her) and each of the doctors came to her bedside daily. She was suffering now from such severe shortness of breath that even oxygen round the clock didn't relieve it. Watching one of the doctors walk in, a nurse in the hallway told me, "She's never going to get any better than this. It's just a matter of time." Soon papers were signed and she was moved to one of the hospital's few hospice beds.

My mother stayed in that bed for several weeks, and then she didn't die. Eventually, her doctors decided that while she was by no means well she was at least stable, and they released her from the hospital. "She's precariously balanced," said one of them. "She could die tomorrow, or she could live for quite some time." So home she went. And home is where she is at this moment, peaceful, but less than ever who she used to be.

Once she was home, I caught my breath, and then decided the time had come to bring my reading of Vincent's journals to a close. It was Swinburne time for Vincent, too. For all his willingness to embrace his life up until its last minute, there was now nothing left to embrace. His apartment had no heat, his nerve damage made writing almost impossible, he couldn't stop coughing, and the volunteers didn't come with his food, not that he could swallow, anyhow. He felt like a ghost already, and never more so than on Super Bowl Sunday 1995, January 29. That was the day the San Francisco 49ers beat the San Diego Chargers and the city seemed concentrated on a single thought, which he wasn't thinking.

"No more cough drops," he wrote, eleven days before he died. "Went to Walgreen's. Since the 49ers won, people cheering and celebrating. And I'm sobbing and coughing at a bus stop."

The last time I had witnessed Vincent's dying and death, sitting on my living room floor the day after the carton came, I hadn't really known him. Then, I was like someone lost in an unfamiliar city anxiously looking for signposts. Now, every somber word cast a shadow. Finally, he recognized that he was unable to take care of himself and was able to get to the phone and call Carol to let her know. She came to his apartment bearing gifts —water he couldn't drink, food he couldn't eat.

The rest was brief and inexorable. Angela and Sandra came, Vincent grew weaker, he thought he'd qualify for hospice care. Then he was hospitalized. Finally, Vincent wrote his last line. "I just want to get it over with."

FOR A MONTH AFTER THAT, I didn't do much of anything, except check nervously now and again to see if I had him with me, the way a chronic loser of keys might lightly pat her pocket just to make sure. At the same time, I was also oddly confident that if I lost him or was momentarily unable to conjure his living presence in myself, I could find him again by taking his diary in my hand and rubbing it Aladdin-style. Maybe that's why he'd left his diaries to me—to guarantee he could always be found. And the picture of himself in the blue windbreaker— "soon all I will be will be a photo"—I thought maybe he'd stuck it in his diary to give me another way of locating him. Photographs, the right ones anyhow, were also doorways. He had used them himself to get to Eddy and Ronny and Ruffin and the others.

One day I was ready to write. That morning, I piled all twelve volumes of Vincent's diaries on the floor near my desk. Then, feeling awkward but game, I taped two photographs of Vincent to the left side of my computer monitor and a third to the right side so he'd be right there whenever I entered into this world, this story, where he and I now coexisted.

The first photograph I chose was the one I had found in his 1994 diary the day after the postman delivered the carton—it shows the man in the blue windbreaker with the mustache, the nose, and the dark glasses. This is the hidden man, the man who won't tell, the man who was afraid to leave me his diaries at all.

The second is a photo from Adrienne that arrived with a yellow Post-it saying "This is Jimmy at a Gay Day Rally." He is again in sunglasses, half smiling, half squinting. The sun shows off the highlights in his hair, and he's wearing a blue and white tank top that shows his lean and muscular chest and upper arms. Behind the dark glasses, though, he's worried, and I know it. The photo is stamped "June 1988" on the back, and Vincent fears that the small mark on his right forearm is a lesion. It is just before Dr. Raszyl tells Vincent he is right. This is the man who left me his diaries so I could save him from disappearing.

The third picture is Vincent at Christmastime, an iced gingerbread house on a piano behind him, a red candle with a golden flame resting on a sprig of green pine. This is the man who is heir to the boy who was outraged by the ending to "The Gift of the Magi" in that long-ago Brooklyn classroom. This is the man who gave me his diaries as a gift.

In all the photos I see the boy I once knew and the man he became, a flawed but decent man whom I grew to care about in a more complicated way than I had ever cared about the boy.

What Vincent wanted from Carol once she knew that he hadn't long to live was for her to treat him just as she always had. To me that meant he didn't want to be regarded differently now that he was dead either. He didn't want to become Aunt Roberta imprisoned in her heart-shaped cage. Whatever I wrote about him, it was not going to be a eulogy or an elegy either. I think what Vincent wanted was for me to find him in his words, even between the lines. Then he wanted me to write him a story he could live in just as I had once told him I might. He would be the star, and at the end, I would leave him alive, recognizable and recognized. Another ending, just what he wanted for the couple in O. Henry's story so long ago.

DURING VINCENT'S LAST WEEK in Paris, shortly before his New Utrecht reunion, he set out to enjoy the city. It was a mild week in October, a good day for strolling. He ambled through the Luxembourg Gardens looking for, and finding, the spot where he'd once taken a photograph that hung on a wall in his apartment. He window-shopped in the Place des Vosages and strolled the Champs-Elysées. He stopped to eat at Burger King.

Soon he was ready to be off again. "Decided to go to Cemetiere du Pere-Lachaise," he wrote. "A little strange being in a cemetery. Oscar Wilde, Sarah Bernhardt, Gertrude Stein & Jim Morrison. People were partying on Jim's grave. It was eerie seeing the name 'Jim' written all over the place. Weather was perfect. Took pictures." Vincent had his blue travel diary with him, a gift from Sharon. He carried it in the backpack he always slung over his shoulder on his day trips. Toward the end of his visit to Morrison's grave, he knelt down and picked two newly fallen leaves up off the ground. He took out his diary and placed the leaves inside, which is where I found them. "Did not want to take anything connected with death," he explained, "so took two leaves for diary." Then he moved on to his future, knowing we'd catch up with him on a perfect fall day in Paris.

Afterword

⸺◦⸺

What force is there in the thing given
Which compels the recipient to make a return?

—Marcel Mauss
The Gift

When Vincent left me his diaries, those who knew of it were fascinated by the mysterious extravagance of his bequest. But not everyone thought of it as a gift. I was asked whether these diaries at my door made me angry. Didn't I feel burdened by the responsibility Vincent had thrust upon me without asking? Didn't I resent the time it would take, and did take, even to read his diaries?

Somehow, I never thought of the diaries as anything *but* a gift: their arrival took its meaning from its place in a sequence of events that began for me with "The Gift of the Magi" and from a classroom conversation about giving, receiving, and the irony of gain in the face of loss. Besides, for twenty-five years I'd been periodically asking Vincent to tell me about his life. These diaries, all 3,500 pages of them, were his answer.

They were a gift in another way, too. Though Vincent got to know me outside of the classroom, in his deepest sense of me—that is, in his dreams—I remained his teacher. For the most part, teachers work in the dark, offering what they can—something beyond how to write an essay or analyze a short story—never quite knowing if their offer is received or what, if anything, the recipient may make of it later on. In this ignorance of results, teachers are unlike doctors or lawyers or bricklayers, one of whom told Studs Terkel how much satisfaction he got every time he passed one of his buildings and saw his bricks, still there doing their part. When Vincent sent me his diaries, he was letting me know there was an outcome. When I was a student, I was very much affected by three teachers—Mrs. Rappaport in third grade, Miss Tannenbaum in high school, and Professor Robinton in college—but only my college professor ever had the slightest notion of her importance, though I still think of all three of them. As for my other two teachers, unfortunately but not surprisingly, I didn't know how significant they were until years later, so how could they have known?

Vincent not only told me about his life after my class, but in leaving me his diaries, he offered me the opportunity, even compelled me, to think about my own life in light of his. In that way, my experience with him didn't "happen" until long after the fact, which is what I understand Eudora Welty to mean when she talks about the inextricable two-way relationship between remembering and discovering. This Möbius strip of memory informed by discovery informed by memory is the story I have been "compelled" to tell.

From the beginning, Vincent was a gift giver who cared about giving the right gift. Whatever else was on his mind, he wanted the diaries to be the right gift for me. And they were, in ways he couldn't have known. The best gifts are not ornamental but those that can be used. And use Vincent's diaries I did. Through them, I understood in a way I had never articulated to myself how ill-equipped I was to deal with death and loss. Just like Vincent. In watching him, at the eleventh hour of his life, learn to manage loss and grief, I saw how I might manage both better myself, along the way redeeming past losses and preparing for one to come. At the end, I had developed a relationship to a man I had never really known and grasped for the first time that a life can open up even as it's closing down. I learned, too, that to let the dead live you must first let the dead die, and further that there is a terrain beyond mourning, terrain I had never known was even part of the landscape. Through

Vincent, I came to understand in a way I hope I have conveyed that one person's relationship to another—Vincent's to Eddy, mine to Vincent—can evolve and grow not only in the face of death but beyond.

In the end, Vincent taught me as much as I ever taught him. Like all teachers, he will never know exactly what he offered. But it was a gift. The proof is the return.

Acknowledgments

When I began to read Vincent's diaries, I had no idea where they would lead me or that it would take me five years to get there. Throughout, I was lucky enough to have astute and generous people close to me who helped me find my way with encouragement, insights, provocative questions, and even a willingness to read yet another draft without audible sighing. For these ministrations, I would like to thank Joanne Aidala, Phima Engelstein, Reamy Jansen, Elliott Lee, and Cynthia Macdonald. It has also been a great pleasure to work with my editor, Elisabeth Scharlatt, on a second project and I thank her once again for her deft and perceptive curiosity which kept me curious and kept me working.

Many other people helped me as readers, or experts, or title-finders. For their gifts in time and responsiveness, I would like to thank: Ann Banks, Leslie Barnes, Donna Bassin, Gail Belsky, Jessica Benjamin, Pat Berry, Liz Birge, Ellen Cantarow, Marion Castellucci, Bob Clyman, Candy Cooper, Lynne Cusack-Tosone, Alice Elliott Dark, Cindy Handler, Diane Harris, Joy Harris, Carole deChellis Hill, Carole and Geoff Howard, Virginia Jerome, Christina Baker Kline, Devon McNamara, Diane McWhorter, Scott Muldoon, Ellen Pall, Steve Posin, Barbara Ridge, Sue Saperstein, Pamela Satran, Abby Schultz, Jill Smolowe, Laura Shapiro, Ann Solomon, Nancy Star, Annalyn Swan, Susan Vaughan, Christine Vogel, Elisabeth Werby, and Deb Wasser. For his kind eye, my thanks to Ed Lynch. My thanks go, too, to the students in my Spring 2001 "First Person Journalism" course at Fordham University for reading the opening pages of this work and offering suggestions and observations that were of definite use. I also thank my students Eric Andersson, Paul Hagen, and Lisa Larkin for reading my final draft and for their feedback.

I am also indebted to those whose contributions allowed me time to work. I would like to thank the administration at Fordham University for awarding me a Faculty Fellowship during Fall 2000, which allowed me time free of all academic responsibilities. Also, without Joan Morris, Mary Radigan, Joan Nelson, Cecilly Telpha, and the staff of the Jacob Terlow Hospice—all of whom take such tender care of my mother, Aurora Stone—I could never have found the time or peace of mind to finish this manuscript.

In a category all their own are Vincent's sisters, Angela, Adrienne, and Sandra, who supported this venture because they believed it was what their brother wanted. I want to thank them for the complete freedom they allowed me in shaping the manuscript, though it includes material they might have preferred omitted. It reflects the love and acceptance they accorded Vincent thoughout his life. Thanks also to Vincent's friends Joey Langweiler, Carol Sebastian, and Sharon D'Amato for their insights about Vincent and their explanations of diary entries that would otherwise have remained baffling.

Finally for their patience during my years of preoccupation, I thank my family.

When Vincent died, he left his books to the San Francisco Public Library. His diaries are now permanently housed there as well, available to researchers in the San Francisco History Room as part of the James C. Hormel Gay and Lesbian Center at the library's main branch.